What others are saying about
Crooked Sidewalks

"In his book, Ron quotes an Old Persian Proverb that says: 'He who knows and knows that he knows, is wise. Follow him.' His insightful and exciting trip through life proves that Ron knows that he knows, and his life is living proof that we should follow him."

Chuck Whitlock
Best Selling Author, Television Personality

"In his book, Ron speaks of wisdom and its applications. After diving into the book, I couldn't put it down. It was as if Ron knew what I needed to read, so many life lessons that applied to me. We are always taught that the shortest distance between two points is a straight line. Ron's words will challenge and encourage you to look for the life's "Crooked Sidewalks" because around every curve, there is a new adventure or something of value you don't want to miss."

Les "PeeWee" Harrison
Author, Speaker, Harlem All-Stars

"Crooked Sidewalks is an entertaining and very personal jaunt down memory lane for the author and his family. It's a collection of experiences and life stories, not unlike many shared by most people, but the difference is that the author took the time to write it down (something we all have said we are going to do 'some day') and to share it with all and to gift us with the vicarious thrill of his experiences while at the same time, reminding us all of our own adventures in life and the value they brought to our existence. Ron Carr's writing style is whimsical, breezy, warm and from the heart. It makes for an easy and enjoyable read and feels like a day of catching up and swapping stories with an old friend. Crooked Sidewalks is not just an acknowledgement to family and friends he has made over his lifetime, but is also a love letter to God to whom the author gives glory to throughout his book. I highly recommend Crooked Sidewalks for those quiet times that most of us look forward to spending on the couch on a lazy afternoon away from our normal fast paced routines to enjoy being 'alone' and totally lost in our thoughts without any outside stimulation or

interference. I found Crooked Sidewalks to be positive, incredibly open-hearted and authentic, encouraging and inspirational. Well done, Ron."

Esmond Chung
Actor, Entertainer, Entrepreneur

"Crooked Sidewalks" takes the reader on a meandering, introspective and perceptive journey, filled with insights that, if personally applied, will make the journey so much more fulfilling and enjoyable. From the first page, I found myself caught up in this unique pilgrimage with Ron, suddenly stumbling upon those insightful "Aha!" moments. It's an enjoyable read, the underlying message always leading the reader down the right path!

Joe Noland - Commissioner
The Salvation Army
Author, Executive Producer

"A thoroughly entertaining, educational, and delightfully woven tapestry of heart-warming stories, inspiring the hope that many, many more miles of 'Crooked Sidewalks' vignettes will be made available for sharing and exploring."

James Townley - Captain, USCG(r)

"A good memoir is both entertaining and enlightening, offering insight into the life and times of the author. After reading Crooked Sidewalks, the words 'faith,' 'hope' and 'character' come to mind. In a world that needs much more of all three it is both refreshing and fun to read about a man honest enough to show his softer side while talking about the most macho of topics, including military service, athletic pursuits, and leadership in business and family. Crooked Sidewalks shines with sincerity and is filled with memorable recollections and sage advice from someone who believes that everyone has a story to tell. Thank goodness he took the time to tell his own!"

"Ron Carr's sometimes hilarious and often inspired reflections will leave you wanting to read more. For someone not as fortunate as I am to be able to call Ron both a colleague and a friend, this collection of stories from his life reveals him to be a man of humor, humility and most of all, faith--faith in Family, Country and God. And best of all, it's fun to read!"

Marilyn Clint - Author, COO,
Portland Rose Festival Foundation

CROOKED SIDEWALKS

Life Lessons Learned

RONALD P. CARR

BALBOA.
PRESS
A DIVISION OF HAY HOUSE

Scripture taken from the New King James Version. Copyright © 1979, 1980, 1982 by Thomas Nelson, Inc. Used by permission. All rights reserved.

Balboa Press books may be ordered through booksellers or by contacting:

Balboa Press
A Division of Hay House
1663 Liberty Drive
Bloomington, IN 47403
www.balboapress.com
1 (877) 407-4847

Because of the dynamic nature of the Internet, any web addresses or links contained in this book may have changed since publication and may no longer be valid. The views expressed in this work are solely those of the author and do not necessarily reflect the views of the publisher, and the publisher hereby disclaims any responsibility for them.

The author of this book does not dispense medical advice or prescribe the use of any technique as a form of treatment for physical, emotional, or medical problems without the advice of a physician, either directly or indirectly. The intent of the author is only to offer information of a general nature to help you in your quest for emotional and spiritual well-being. In the event you use any of the information in this book for yourself, which is your constitutional right, the author and the publisher assume no responsibility for your actions.

Any people depicted in stock imagery provided by Getty Images are models, and such images are being used for illustrative purposes only. Certain stock imagery © Getty Images.

Print information available on the last page.

ISBN: 978-1-9822-2302-1 (sc)
ISBN: 978-1-9822-2303-8 (e)

Balboa Press rev. date: 03/11/2019

Dedication

This book is dedicated to Jan, my wife and life partner, for all her love, patience, caring and support she has given me throughout our forty plus years together as husband and wife. She has also provided unconditional encouragement and support throughout the completion of this book. I am so blessed that God gave her to me, or maybe me to her. Regardless, Jan, you mean the world to me and you have taught me so much, while giving so much, including my wonderful children, daughters Kristie and Kelly, and my son, James.

Thank you for your love and for all the great memories we share.

Foreword

Ron Carr has lived a long and successful life. As a personal friend of his for over half a century, I can tell you that he is a man who has largely gotten it right. If one, as a high school student, was to make a list of really important things to "achieve" in life, fast forward 50 years and look back, Ron is one of the few who could do so with an earned sense of pride. He is still married to his high school sweetheart Jan, has countless friends, has produced a fine family which looks a lot like him and, fortunately, more like Jan. He has traveled the world, known famous people, tasted more than a few careers and positively affected many of the lives of those around him.

Ron makes a basic assertion that "everyone has a story and most are never told", attempts to tell his own, and in the process tells the story of countless others. ***Crooked Sidewalks*** is a carefully crafted collection of a lifetime's worth of encounters, impressions, and observations about people, life and how it is lived. It is the book you and I should have written but either didn't have the time or were not insightful enough to notice what surrounds us every day.

Ron is not a man to miss much. It is obvious that he feels as much as he notices. The anecdotal "mini-stories" sprinkled throughout the book are thoughtful and often humorously entertaining. A philosophy of goodness permeates every page. Don't be surprised if you find a bit of yourself or someone you love in these slices of life.

It is perhaps a good thing that not everyone tells their story. However, in these pages, you'll find a story well told of a life well lived.

Walt Waggener
Business Man and Life Long Friend

Introduction

I should state right up front that it is my personal belief that each and every one of us is put here on this earth for a purpose. I may not know what my purpose is, but at some time in my life, I may figure it out. I also very strongly believe that every life is a story and the story is specific to each person, each being, and each soul. There is a beginning, which starts even before we are born, and there is an end on the day that we pass away. Everything that happens in between is "the story" of that life.

In Crooked Sidewalks, the title of this book, as well as the first chapter, I share a very important principle of life which has taken me years to learn. I believe it all relates to how we look at life. I also believe, as I have heard on many occasions that "our life is God's gift to us, and what we do with that life is our gift back to God." In my world, I believe it.

So, life happens! I have thought about this for many years, as have many others, I am sure. Every life is a story, or as I like to think of it, every life is a book that unfolds over time. The book is made up of chapters, each chapter being a period of time, a certain event, a personal relationship or something that defines or leads to what happens next, or a change of direction on our journey. Some chapters may be short, others may be long. Some are exciting and some may be seriously boring. These chapters can be filled with joy and happiness and some may be filled with sorrow, pain and despair. Some are good and some are bad, or somewhere in between. Some are magical, some inspirational, and some are tragedies.

From the time of our birth, and even before, we are impacted by our surroundings, our environment, relations or interactions with those we come in contact with. Some circumstances we have control over, while there are many others we have no control over. We are being carried downstream in a rushing river with life happening all around us and around every bend. It can be extremely exciting or it can be extremely terrifying. Regardless, it is life and the story of our journey.

Another point I choose to believe is that every person and every life is important and is part of our history of humanity. Therefore, I also believe every life is worthy of a book. Unfortunately, not everyone's life story is captured and chronicled in the form of a book, although that would be a wonderful thing. Since every life matters, a book about that life would do so much to help us and others learn about our family, our history and our efforts to make the world a better place. We can learn from our failures and successes and share with others, while also learning from others who share their story with us. It may also help us when we contemplate questions like, "Who am I" or, "Why do I exist" or, in the grand scheme of things, "What is my purpose here on earth?" Lord knows, I don't have all the answers, but I have learned a few things along the way.

My story, represented by the chapters of this book, is just one story in billions in all the history of mankind. It is no more special or less special than anyone else's. What does make it special to me is that it is mine.

They tell me that with age, one gains wisdom. I have been advised by those more elderly than me, that the wisdom one gains does not guarantee any diminishment of misjudgments. The bad news, they tell me, is that I will still make mistakes. The good news is that I will make them more slowly. This book, I am certain, is not one of them.

These are just a few of many stories or chapters in my life. I hope they will share with you some insights, and they will encourage you on your own journey in understanding the various chapters of your own book. As I have journeyed through my life, I've had my ups and downs, my wins and my losses, even a few memorable and worthy achievements. Realistically, though, my life is not that so different from a lot of people and, when all is said and done and with all that has happened, I can rejoice in the fact that I am still alive. Apparently, God isn't done with me yet. So, I can celebrate that fact and continue to enjoy my journey and keep moving forward. I wish you the very best in your own journey as you realize you too are special.

Ronald Carr

Contents

Foreword.. vii
Introduction.. ix

Crooked Sidewalks.. 1
Mt. Fuji... 5
He's Crazy..11
Push Through the Stall..17
Almost Gone Forever 21
Navigator, where are we? 27
Jan and the Monkee 33
The Greater Sin 39
Hit the Deck 43
Did I ever tell you the story?... 47
One Day 51
My Wife for Life 55
I Love Julia Roberts...61
Turn In That Ticket 65
Thrift Store Treasures 69
It's Just A Penny 77
Not All Green Lights 81
Down From the Mountain Top... 85
Crossing the Line 89
One, Two Three…Too Late 95
Ain't No Big Ting Bruddah!... 99
For Love of the Game 107
Mamma My Angel... 111
Like A Rose..117

About the Author...131

Old Persian Proverb

He who knows not, and knows not that he knows not,
is a fool, shun him.

He who knows not, and knows that he knows not,
is a student, teach him.

*He who knows, and knows **not** that he knows,*
is asleep, wake him.

He who knows, and knows that he knows,
is wise, follow him.

Crooked Sidewalks

"Life is simultaneously a journey, a destination and a state of mind."

T.S. Elliott

I love these beautiful Sunday afternoons, especially the ones that are blue, bright and clear, but with a few clouds dotting the sky. Depending on the wind and the atmospheric influences, the clouds take on such unique and expressive shapes. The blueness of the sky behind them really helps create the depth and richness of the vast unknown, while accentuating the shape of each cloud. It's probably irrelevant here, but my favorite color is blue, and when the sky is such a rich, deep blue, it lifts my spirit and suggests unlimited possibilities that life has to offer.

I was on my way to attend a concert of the Southwest Washington Wind Symphony, an incredibly talented assembly of music educators who not only teach their students, but they lead by example and maintain their musical talents. Their performances are always well-themed, exquisitely performed and provide a rich cultural experience in their home town of Vancouver, Washington. And, every concert is free to the general public, a wonderful gesture of giving back to their community and the families of the students they teach. Their concerts are always a treat and a place for me to lose myself in the wonder of the music.

It only takes me about fifteen minutes from my house to drive the distance to Union High School in Vancouver where the symphony performs. When I left the freeway and headed north on a hundred and ninety second, I became aware of all the new construction and the developing landscape along the way. What struck me at that moment was how all of the new sidewalks were crooked. Well, not exactly crooked, but not straight. I was noticing how the developers had intentionally made the sidewalks to meander back and forth in the direction up the street. This was different from what I had become accustomed to throughout my life, and I liked it.

I used to do a lot of walking, usually to get from one place to another, especially as a kid when I had no other means of transportation. Back then, and even until recently, it seemed that the sidewalks were straight and framed the streets, which was especially noticeable in the city.

When I walked from my home the six miles to my dad's office, as far as I could see, the sidewalks were straight. So, for the most part, I was looking straight ahead as I made my trek, with minimal interest of what was going on around me. My objective was to get to my dad's office for whatever reason, as quickly as I could. I was focused on getting there and really didn't spend any time surveying my surroundings. I'm sure I missed a lot. I know I must have walked by a few hundred store fronts, but couldn't really remember then or now, what they were if you asked me. I don't even remember if there were trees or parks to distract me on my way. Now that I think about it, maybe that was unusual for a kid.

Getting back to today, I was especially interested in the way the sidewalks were no longer straight, but wandered along the road, weaving in and around trees, bus stops, small mounds of grass and other scenic distractions. It dawned on me what a great idea this new approach is for anyone using the sidewalk as their path along the way. Instead of walking down an endless sidewalk focused on the distance ahead of me, I am forced to follow the wandering sidewalk and see the landscape along the way. The winding path causes me to look to the right and see the trees, flowers and bushes making up the scenery. Then, as the sidewalk curves back to the left, I'm forced to look in another direction and see the sights situated there.

This approach causes me to slow down and enjoy the beauty that is built into and surrounds the pathway. Because of the winding sidewalk, I'm no longer able to look a long distance ahead of me. In fact, I'm somewhat limited to what I am able to see any farther than half a block away. More importantly, I am seeing things that I would have otherwise walked by without even acknowledging their existence.

I've heard it said many times in a variety of ways, but it still comes out to express the same truth. It's not the destination that brings the greatest value of the trip, but it's the experiences enjoyed along the way. That is so true.

We often times get so caught up in life and trying to keep pace with the speed with which we have to move in this day and age, and it's only getting faster, that we miss so much of what life has to offer. There are so many things we are going to get around to doing, some day, when we have more time or when circumstances change, yet very rarely do we get to that point as we'd thought. There is always something else to do. Too many times, and too late in life, we realize how much we have missed and what we could have done. I'm speaking from experience.

For too many years, I was so focused on my career thinking that I would work really hard and fast, and I would get everything to a point when I could back off and have more time for myself, my other interests, and most important, for my family.

After many years of pursuing that plan, I came to the realization of how much I had missed and would never be able to re-capture. Those opportunities and experiences were lost forever. Those things I missed with my two daughters and son would be regrets that I would have to live with for the rest of my life. I also realized that although those times were lost, I could start today to create new experiences and memories for the rest of my life. I vowed that I would no longer let my busy-ness get in the way of what is most important. My life and my loved ones are most important, and everything else is secondary.

When I am enjoying my life, I am so much more prepared to give to everyone else and help them enjoy their lives. Zig Ziglar has always said: "You can get everything you want in life by helping others to get what they want."

We must evaluate our own busy-ness and intentionally decide what is most important in our life. Then, we need to make the necessary changes to put our priorities in their proper place. This is what we can do, and need to do, today. This is the only thing we have control over.

Those crooked sidewalks got my attention today and really reminded me so much about taking the time to enjoy the things of life along the journey. I've heard it before, but occasionally, we need to be reminded.

While you're traveling through life, don't miss a thing. See all you can see and experience all you can experience. You will be much happier and your life will be richer for it. I went on to enjoy the symphony with an enriched attitude and took in the full measure of the music experienced and the memories enhanced. Wow! What a great day.

Mt. Fuji

I was lying in bed in a naval hospital in Yokosuka, Japan. It was mid-August nearing the end of my tour aboard the USS Richard B Anderson, a naval destroyer I was assigned to for my Viet Nam service. I was waiting for the doctor to release me from the hospital so I could get back to my ship, and to my wife, Jan. She had joined me in Japan after I'd completed my engineering school in San Diego the previous year. The day before, I'd had surgery on my right wrist to remove a ganglion, and Jan was coming to the hospital to help me check out.

The ganglion had grown to the size of a small walnut on my wrist and was making it difficult, and painful, even to do pushups. It was time to do something about it, so I reported to sick bay to check with the corpsman to see what needed to be done. The corpsman shared with me that there were two ways to get rid of a ganglion. One was to have surgery to have it cut out of my wrist. The other way, which seemed to create the most excitement in his eyes, was for me to lay my arm flat on the table, ganglion side up. That was my part. His part was to take a big phone book or something comparable, and slam it down on my wrist really hard, causing the ganglion to burst and scatter in my system. He was enjoying the prospect too much, and with further investigation, in considering my options, I learned that the phone book method didn't guarantee the ganglion would be gone for good. It could return. I wasn't interested in an annual wrist stomping attack on my body, so I opted for surgery. Life is full of decisions, and it is important to evaluate all our options. Although not an instant fix without pain or recovery time, I chose surgery as the best choice for the long term benefit for my wrist.

The surgery was successful and I was waiting to be released. In the meantime, one of the other officers from the ship stopped in to let me know there was a group planning to climb Mt. Fuji and was leaving that afternoon and wanted to know if I was going to go. Since it was the last weekend during the Mt. Fuji climbing season that the ship would be in port, I said yes. I knew I would never have another chance to make that climb since I would be transferred to another ship in the next month or so. That could take me back to the states or to some other station around the world.

While Jan was waiting with me in my hospital room until the doctor could come by and clear me to go home, I told her what I was planning to do. She said there was no way, the day after surgery, that I should be climbing a mountain. We discussed it, sort of, and the decision was that we would talk to the doctor and see what he recommended.

The doctor finally showed up, and Jan and I each had a chance to make our case for climbing Mt Fuji, or not. I wanted to go, and she didn't think I should. Normally, she would be okay with it, but was concerned if I would be able to handle the climb the day after surgery. The doctor reminded me that I had a body full of anesthesia and it would take about a week for it to completely be out of my system. He also pointed out that I would be somewhat weak.

However, he then surprised us both by telling me that as long as I took my time and paced myself, I would probably be just fine. So, he had no objection to my making the climb. Besides, I had a number of my shipmates going as well, and they could help me if I needed it.

Based on the doctor's "OK", Jan agreed to take me back to the house, and then helped me put a backpack together of things I would need for the climb, including a sleeping bag, extra socks, a sweatshirt, and a supply of sandwiches and water to drink. At 4:00 pm, a couple of my fellow officers from the ship picked me up and we headed to Mt Fuji.

We arrived at Station five, the starting point that would make it possible for us to reach the summit by sunrise. We could have started at lower levels, but were restricted by time. We became a few among many who were also making the pilgrimmage. The climb itself, being a tradition and spiritual trek each year for many of the Japanese people, was relatively easy. It was pretty much consistent cutbacks all the way up the mountain. The challenge was that it was a long ways to the summit and the constant incline required continual effort, especially as we got farther up the mountain and the air became thinner.

I learned that the elevation of Mt. Fuji is twelve thousand, three hundred and sixty-five feet. It's easy to remember since there are twelve months in a year, and three hundred and sixty-five days in the same year, not counting each leap year. And now that I've shared that piece of information with you in this easy-to-remember manner, you will likely never forget this little bit of trivia to share with your friends. It's easy to remember that way. I also learned that the climb is a personal commitment for many Japanese, with the goal of arriving at the summit in time to see the sunrise. That was also my goal for this climb.

Before heading up the mountain, we had an opportunity to purchase a walking stick, and the merchant burned a symbol near the middle of the stick to indicate where we started our climb. That was station number five. Then, each time we reached a new station level, we could spend a few yen and have that station brand burned onto the stick in the next position up. When we arrived at station eight at midnight, I had my walking stick branded again, and then I settled in to eat some sandwiches Jan prepared, climbed in my sleeping bag for some rest. It was a short night.

We woke up at three o'clock in the morning, packed up our gear and continued our climb. We only had a few hours to reach the summit so we had to get going at a steady and decent pace to be sure to make the summit in time for the sunrise. I didn't realize what I was in for and that it was going to take a real commitment to be there in time.

We had passed the last station before the summit with about an hour to go before sunrise, and by now, I was really feeling the drain on my body. The doctor was right. I'm sure it was a combination of the anesthesia in my system, the increasing altitude and thinning air, the strain and challenge of the climb, and the need to push myself to arrive at the summit. I was drained and seriously wondered if I was ever going to get there at all, let alone get to the top in time to see the sunrise. The backpack was weighing on me, and my legs were feeling the pain. The elevation and limited air was making me work harder just to keep breathing. It was cold, but I didn't feel it because I was working so hard. I was sweating, so I took my coat off to give me some relief and tied it around my waist.

The climb was taking its toll on my strength and endurance. I finally got to the point where I had to make each cutback an individual goal and required everything I had just to get to the next one. I was now seriously concerned if I could make it and was considering what an embarrassment it would be to quit. It was at that point that something occurred that completely changed my perspective and gave me that inner strength and drive that I would need to reach the summit, and do it before the sun came up.

In my pain and weakness, my first reaction to what I saw was more like adding insult to injury. As I stopped periodically at the end of each cutback, I noticed a number of little old Japanese women who were making their trek along with me. I was twenty-five years of age at the time, and based on my best guess, many of these graceful ladies were two to three times my age. They were moving slow and steady and were passing me as I stopped to catch my breath. I don't think their climb was any less demanding than mine, but they just kept their slow and steady movement forward to reach the top and experience whatever it was to be when they reached it.

Maybe, at that point, I was being somewhat put to shame, maybe not. But, I was challenged and inspired to go on. I continued through the next cutback, and then the next, and then the next. I was never sure how many more I had to complete, but the clock was ticking and I knew I had to be close. Finally, when I reached the top of another cutback length, I was there. I saw the ground level out, my shipmates waiting for me, and I knew I had reached the summit. I was standing at the lighter side of dark, where it is still gray, but no longer night. The sun hadn't yet broken over the distant edge of the world below. I'd made it and reached the top with only minutes to spare.

I took a deep breath and heaved a sigh of relief as I walked toward the edge and waited for the sun. As it crested and burst its rays toward us, I felt exhilaration of the accomplishment and at the same time, a spirit of peace and calm. It was done and I was grateful I'd had the chance to experience this day standing on the summit of the beautiful and majestic Mt. Fuji.

After taking in the beauty, I walked over to another little merchant to have the last of the brands burned onto my walking stick. This time, the brand was tinted red to mean I'd reached the top. I joined my buddies and enjoyed a warm bowl of soup. I don't know what it was, but it tasted so good. When we finished, we started down the mountain. I was no longer tired, weak or drained. All the energy came back with the win of reaching the summit, in spite of the challenges.

For me, this was an opportunity of a lifetime and perhaps, the only time I would be able to experience this climb. I learned years earlier that if you are presented with an opportunity to experience something new, even if the circumstances aren't necessarily ideal or perfect in every way, it is worth making the decision to go for it. Like Nike's motto says, "Just Do It!" So I did, and it was worth all the pain, weakness and sore muscles to give it a try. I did it, and it has been just one of the many experiences and memories I can hold on to forever. It was good. No, it was great!

He's Crazy
What am I doing here?

"Pain is inevitable; suffering is optional."

H. White

It was in the summer between my junior and senior years of college. I had committed to a special Navy program for prospective candidates for receiving training leading to a Navy commission. The draft was in full swing and Viet Nam was well under way and escalating.

It had always been my desire to follow in my father and uncle's footsteps and serve my country in the military. My dad was a Petty Officer Corpsman in the Navy during World War II. My uncles were in the Army and the Marines, so military service ran deep in my family. It only made sense to me that if I was going to serve, I would rather do it as an officer and be in a position to lead. The OCS (Officer Candidate School) program gave me the opportunity to continue my college education while attending OCS training in the summer prior to my senior year, and then another summer following graduation.

During the school year, I attended weekly training at the local Reserve Center in Pomona, California. I was getting acclimated to the military, but really had no idea what was in store when I arrived at Navy OCS.

We were brand new recruits, brand new officer candidates when we arrived at the US Navy Officer Candidate School in Newport, Rhode Island. It was hot and humid and we were just beginning our two and half months of first summer training. New candidates arrived in all sorts of shapes, sizes and colors and we were each dressed in what we thought

11

was the appropriate attire for arriving at the school. For me it was another one of those questions of "What was I thinking?"

When I stepped off the bus into the heat and humidity of Newport, RI, I was wearing the only suit I had, and in retrospect, I was wondering why I was wearing a suit at all? In addition, just a few days before leaving my home for OCS, I made sure I went and got a haircut. I really hadn't thought that through. One of the first things they did as they marched us from check-in station to station, was to go to a row of barbers to have our heads shaved. I was still in my black suit, sweating profusely, and the barber only sort of brushed the hair off my shoulders. I must have looked ridiculous in a suit in this weather with a newly shaved head. The only redeeming factor for me was that I have a pretty symmetrically perfect looking head.

Heads came in all shapes and sizes, and having all your hair removed really exposes yours. I could only imagine that some of the births of some of those other recruits had to have been extremely painful. It was nearly two hours later before I walked by a mirror and had a chance to sneak a quick look at my shaved white head sitting on top of my black suit, white shirt and tie. I felt ridiculous.

But that was only the beginning.

After we were all checked in, receiving our allotment of uniforms, almost having a meal, and being assigned to our rooms, "Hell Week" began in earnest. This was just the first week we had to survive to continue moving forward in our training. The purpose of this week was to break us down quickly from being civilians before starting the process of building us up into Navy ready officer candidates.

I understood this, so the goal for me, as I'm sure each person had his own way of coping, was to keep going through all the orders and demands, both physically and mentally, and come out the other end intact, and still know who I am. They let us know we could quit any time and "go home to our mommies." They tried to push us through what sometimes seemed like unreasonable and impossible demands. The stress was tremendous and I believe beyond what any of us had experienced before.

They put us through our paces with every calisthenics known to man at the time, but I think they were working on creating new ones to test us. We were late to bed and early to rise. I don't think we were actually sleep deprived, but they really pushed the limits. They ran us through obstacle courses and then ran us some more just to run us.

The breaks were far and few between, and when we weren't exercising, we were cleaning something whether it was our shoes, our rooms, the hallways, bathrooms or any other area that had already been cleaned a hundred times before. We didn't dig holes in the ground, but the process reminded me of Paul Newman as Cool Hand Luke. Remember how when in prison, Luke had to dig a hole. Once it was dug, he was accused of digging it in the wrong place, so he had to fill it in and then dig another hole someplace else.

The Navy wasn't that cruel, but they made sure we didn't have a chance to rest or have any time to ourselves. It was their intent to find out what we were made of. They pushed us to our physical limits and then demanded more. It didn't matter how many times you threw up, and the only time you were allowed to stop is when you collapsed. A corpsman was always nearby to assist if needed.

Throughout the whole week, they kept reminding us that we were 'nothing' and certainly <u>not</u> officer candidate material unless we completed this week. They demanded perfection in maintaining inspection-ready uniforms, including perfectly shined shoes. There could not be a mark, a smudge, a spot or even a piece of lint anywhere on our uniform. That would surely guarantee, forgive my language, the "ass-chewing" of our life to this point, and they pretty much implied that was going to happen anyway. Our instructors were relentless in their demands for "attention to detail." It seemed to be part of every sentence of every command. Our lives depended on it. Our survival depended on it, and our staying in the program depended on it. Each time something was accomplished, some instructor would add the command, "that and better will do!"

The week was taking its toll on everyone, including me. It felt endless and there seemed to always be an upper classman with bad breath in my face, yelling some command laced with a tirade of profanities. As most of us did, we stared directly ahead and took whatever they had to give us, right or wrong, reasonable or not. The one thing for me that kept me going was the fact that there was an end date. At the end of the week, ready or not, we would have a final inspection, the results of which would determine if we would continue in the training, or head for home. The person that was going to make the final inspection was our Company Commander. We had never seen him or met him, but they assured us he was the meanest and most demanding S.O.B at the school. His specialty was finding the one thing you didn't find or had forgotten, and then he would verbally destroy your very being.

The day finally arrived. The inspection preparation was complete. Our shoes were shined and our uniforms were crisp and spotless. We took turns inspecting each other to make sure we hadn't missed anything.

When you share an experience like this, you become a team of survivors. This is not an individual sport, and looking out for your shipmates was a mantra. A camaraderie was being established that we would appreciate our whole lives, one that is common to all that serve this great country. It is one of the enduring characteristics of being in the service, in the brotherhood. We were as ready as we could be.

We were all lined up in our barracks hallway, standing at ease with our backs to the wall. Just before the commander walked in, someone shouted "ATTENN-HUTT!" We all snapped to attention, focused and stood ready for whatever was to come. When this guy walked in, he was everything they had promised, which was something related to Satan's spawn. He gave some brief barking comments and then started down the one side and worked his way down and around to the other.

Absolutely no one was immune from his wrath. As he stopped and inspected each candidate and found failure after failure, his intensity grew and his pounding voice became all-consuming. I was sure this guy was not human. I listened to him go on for what seemed like eternity. When he finally stepped in front of me, I braced myself for the barrage, stared straight ahead and did everything within my being to restrain my impulse to choke him and slam his head into the deck. (In the Navy, all floors are decks) He was finally done with me and moved on to the next victim. I think I took a breath for the first time in three minutes.

The harassment and pillage continued for the next twenty minutes. The final straw for me was when the commander became so irate, he grabbed the perfectly constructed cover (hat) from the candidate across the hall, drew his sword and impaled the hat, completely destroying it, tossing it down the hallway and stormed out of the room. I remember clearly the thought that was going through my head at that moment was "He's crazy!

If this is what they turn you into, then I'm not interested." I restrained myself and stood at attention. When the commander was finally gone, the upper classmen came around and said "Congratulations, it's over." They had to say it several times. None of us believed them. We were frozen at attention, scared to death to move.

I finally realized it was true when an upper classman came up to me laughing, pulled my tie out of its perfectly formed position, and said "Relax. It's over. You made it." I breathed out and fought back the tears as all the stress poured from my body and the relief exposed itself with tears swelling up in my eyes. It really was over. I had endured and was now an official US Navy Officer Candidate. I was so relieved, and I was not the only one dealing with tears. We shook hands, hugged and patted each other on the back, recounting what had just happened.

The commander came back into the room and started shaking everyone's hand and giving them his congratulations. I was ready to give him an academy award for his performance. I wished it had been captured on film. After now having been at OCS for two weeks, our reward was to finally be able to call home and speak to our families. It wasn't easy without choking up again, but it was all worth it.

The exhilaration of our survival and achievement was an incredible feeling. In the back of my mind, I could imagine my high school coach saying: "Hang in there", and my dad saying: "Keep your head down, keep going and never give up." Whenever I faced hard times or difficulties, I could also hear my mom saying: "This too shall pass." The other truth echoing inside my head was the old adage that "What doesn't kill you makes you stronger." I became a believer and was determined to focus on those encouragements and I made it through. And, this was only the beginning.

Push Through the Stall

"You don't get to choose how or when you are going to die,
you can only decide on how you are going to live."

Joan Baez

Ever since I was a small child, it had always been my dream to fly. My desire was so strong that I would regularly have dreams that I could fly, unassisted. It wasn't like I was Superman or some other super hero, but I could decide to take off and soar above the ground up to heights of twenty or thirty feet. I was growing up on a farm during those days and I can remember my most vivid dreams of taking off and flying around and over the barn. The feeling was absolutely exhilarating in every sense of the imagination. I couldn't think of anything that felt better than the ability to launch myself into the air and look down at the barn, corrals and orchards below.

That dream stayed with me well into my college years and one day during my junior year, I made the decision to take flying lessons. Not too far from my college, there was an airstrip called Brackett Field. I went over to learn about what was involved and how much money it would cost to have lessons and get my private license. I'm sure the price was reasonable, but it didn't matter to me. I wanted to fly. Between a couple of my scholarships and loans, I was able to put together enough money to start taking lessons. I couldn't have been happier.

First, I had to get my flight physical to make sure I was healthy enough to fly. This is required by law. Then I started taking the ground classes to prepare me for all aspects of flying from the theoretical and practical perspective. It is important to understand how to navigate and get from point A to point B. This was initially learned in a classroom setting.

Finally, the day came when I started my flying lessons with my instructor. He was a patient and experienced man in his mid-fifties and was clearly qualified and experienced to teach me how to take off, fly and land safely, that last part being the most critical in my mind. I once heard someone say, "I love to fly United, and land the same way." We used a small Cessna One Fifty as our trainer. I think it was about as basic an aircraft that you could get into.

One day, when I'd completed seven hours of flight training, we spent the day doing "touch and goes", which are take offs and landings, and then going around and doing it over and over again. Each approach was slightly different, but my confidence was building, and I began to make some very decent landings. As we were about to go around again, I pulled off onto the taxiway, and my instructor told me to stop the plane. I did as directed, at which point he opened the door and got out. My eyes widened and I asked him where he was going? He told me I was going go do, by myself, what we had been doing over the last hour. He said "you are ready for your first solo flight." At the moment, I think he had more confidence in me than I had in myself. However, he was the instructor and I trusted him.

I taxied over to the start of the runway and notified the tower I was ready to take off. I waited for their clearance, shoved the throttle forward and headed down the runway. At the appropriate time I pulled back on the controls and I was airborne. It was such an incredible feeling of freedom and a personal achievement I've never forgotten. I climbed to the appropriate altitude, turned left until I could start my down wind leg, start my decent and continue onto my base leg and then the final approach. The focus is to line up on the runway with a pre-determined touch down point, and time the decent and reduction in power to arrive at the point with a very soft touch of the wheels as they reached the runway. Safely down, I taxied back to the school where my instructor was waiting.

What I didn't know is that my dad had come to pick me up and was there as well when I shut the engine down. He told me he was surprised and a bit concerned when he saw the instructor get out of the aircraft. It was a wonderful feeling to achieve that level of success. When I got out of the plane, my instructor and dad met me. Then another member of the flight school came out and they cut away almost the entire back of my long sleeve dress shirt. I learned this was a long-standing tradition for pilots when they complete their first solo flight. My name and date, and plane number were written on the cloth, and I took it home as a souvenir of this important flying milestone.

My lessons continued for the next few months as I added to my flight time and preparation for the eventual written test to qualify for my license. One of the most personally challenging lessons for me to master, because it was the scariest, was the lesson of learning how to pull out of a stall. It is not only important, but critical. The stall is created when, for whatever reason, there is no longer enough air speed and lift under the wings to keep the plane flying. This causes it to stall, and in essence, fall out of the sky. The sudden and uncontrollable drop is the scariest thing I can ever recall experiencing. The plane is spinning and falling toward the ground. Depending on your elevation, you have to quickly gain control and get your airspeed back up or you are going to impact the ground. One of the main reasons planes crash from stalls is the lack of pilot training and practice for responding to this situation, and the most common causes for the pilot is panic. Our tendency is to try to pull back on the controls and keep the plane flying. It doesn't work without the required airspeed.

My school and instructor made this a regular requirement during the training to practice stalls and build confidence in the pilot to be able to pull out of a stall if it ever occurred. We practiced and practiced, and each time, my stomach jumped into my throat from the fear that I was dealing with. I learned from my instructor that the key to overcoming that fear and regaining my airspeed was to push through the stall.

Instead of pulling back on the controls, I had to face my fear and push the controls forward. This forced the nose of the plane down, albeit toward the ground and allowed it to quickly gain the airspeed it needed for me to again be able to fly and control the plane. "Push through the stall," I said to myself over and over again. "Push through the stall." Eventually I overcame my fear and developed the level of confidence to deal with a stall however it occurs, including intentionally pulling the plane up into a climbing turn to the point where it fell out of the sky to one side or the other. The recovery process was the same. "Push through the stall." I did.

I learned and passed my flight exam and received my flying certificate, or license. It was a good and satisfying day.

That lesson came back to my mind many times throughout my life. "Push through the stall." Regardless of what the challenge was, or the amount of fear that came with it, I knew I had to overcome that fear and again, "push through the stall." In other words, use your training, face the fear head on and regain control of your life. Don't let fear control you.

I've also since heard that FEAR is an acronym for "**F**alse **E**vidence **A**ppearing **R**eal." How many times do we not do something or try something new for fear of failure? Sometimes we don't even start because we are afraid we might fail. Fear paralyzes many people who haven't learned to accept fear as a fact of life, and that through practice we can face our fears and move forward toward our successes. We learn more from our failures than we do from our successes, so I believe we should learn to celebrate our successes and our failures. Face the fact that we are human and we are going to fail some times. That is ok for most things because we can learn from our failures and grow. "It is better to try something and fail than it is to try nothing and succeed." I'm not one to want to try nothing and succeed. I want to "push through the stall" and be responsible for the success that follows. There is so much to gain and enjoy in life if we learn this lesson. Try it. "Push through the stalls" in your life. Let me know how it goes. I'll celebrate with you.

Almost Gone Forever
What was I thinking?

*"Good judgement comes from experience and that
experience grows out of mistakes."*
General Omar Bradley

I had just completed engineering school in San Diego, California and was
on my way back to my ship, the USS Richard B. Anderson DD-786, a
destroyer. At the present time, and for the next year and a half, we were
stationed off the east coast of Viet Nam.

When I'd left for engineering school, there were only two ships along
the coast, mine and one other destroyer. When I returned, there were at
least twenty-seven ships spread north to south along a ten mile stretch just
below the DMZ (de-militarized zone). However, that is another story for
another day.

On my way back to my ship, I was flown into Clark Air Base just
outside of Subic Bay in the Philippines. The Subic Bay Naval base was
where all US ships reported when coming to the Philippines. In order to
get back to the Anderson, I was assigned to another ship, the USS Newport
News, in order to get a ride back to the gun line off the Viet Nam coast.
However, the ship that was to transport me back to the Anderson would
be in port for a few days, so I had a chance to see some of the sites.

I walked out the main gate of the base and headed into Olongapo,
which is the small town just outside the base, a popular place for sailors to
go. I had plenty of time so I just enjoyed walking along the equivalent of
Main Street, looking into the various shops set up along the way to attract

tourists, and in particular, US military men and women. One shop in particular caught my attention.

What attracted me were the beautiful paintings of all sizes and colors displayed on the walls in what was more of a walk-way between buildings than an actual store. These folks were resourceful in using the space they had. I especially enjoyed the variety of seascape paintings of various shades of blue and white on velvet material, very popular in those days.

However, the artwork was wonderful and displayed very well. They also had similar paintings, but with oranges, yellows and gold, suggesting a seascape at sunset. That was the one I chose. It was about three feet by four feet framed in a black and gold style frame. The price was more than reasonable, so I paid the twenty US dollars and planned to carry it back to my quarters. The gentleman who sold it to me offered to package it for shipping so I could mail it back home, and I could pick it up the next day. That worked for me because I was going to be in Subic Bay for a few days before heading back to my ship.

Later that evening while I was having dinner at the Subic Bay Officers Club, we all received notification there was a typhoon headed toward the Philippines, and the ships would be getting underway first thing in the morning. It is always better for a ship to be at sea during heavy weather than to be moored up to a dock and possibly get battered around in port.

Realizing I would be leaving early in the morning, I needed to get back into town and pick up the seascape I had purchased. When, I walked out of the officer's club, it was pouring down rain. I was standing there thinking about how I was going to get to the main gate and into town to pick up my painting, when an older gentleman came out of the club. As we waited, a black car pulled up, and I asked the gentleman if that was his car. When he said "yes", I asked if he would mind giving me a ride out to the main gate. He said, "Sure. Hop in."

His driver drove us to my new friend's home there on the base, and then he turned and directed his driver to take me out to the main gate. I thanked him, and as he walked away, I saw the sign in front of his house which said: "Commanding Officer, Subic Bay Naval Base." Oops! It hadn't dawned on me that this officer was the commander of the base. I was a little embarrassed, but grateful as well. He was certainly "an officer and a gentleman." Thank you Captain, wherever you are.

When I crossed the small bridge into Olongapo, the look of the town had completely changed. While during the day, Main Street is lined with shops, in the evening it turns into bars and bordellos, red lights and all. Women of the night were plentiful and willing to help a sailor meet all his deepest desires. As beautiful and tempting as these women were, my only desire was to collect my painting and return to the base. Oh yes, I am human. I was also happily married to my beautiful and incredible wife, Jan, and for those wondering, I still am to this day.

I was having some trouble finding the exact shop I'd visited during the day time, but finally narrowed it down to what I remembered. As I entered the space between the shops, I told the ladies there I was looking for Mr. Hansen, I think that was his name. He was quickly located and came out to see me. I told him I needed to pick up my painting because I'd be leaving in the morning. He was very congenial and offered to take me out to the place where my painting was being packed.

We found a Jeepney, an old jeep used as a taxi, cleverly decorated in a myriad of colors, trimmings and "bling" to make them attractive to tourists and sailors. We traveled for about twenty-five minutes somewhere out into what I would consider the suburbs of Olongapo. We stopped in front of a shanty house that had cloth material hanging in place of a door. As we stepped into the house, I'm sure someone's home, there were eight Filipino men sitting around in various stages of drunkenness. I was offered a seat on the couch just inside the door as my friend went to somewhere in the back to finish packing up the painting.

They looked at me and smiled, and I nodded back. I don't think they spoke English until one man crawled out from behind a curtain and sat down next to me. He was, as we said in the Navy, several sheets to the wind, or very inebriated, but friendly enough. He did speak English and asked if I would like to have a drink with him. I wasn't about to say no. He seemed to be someone of importance to this group of men because he directed one to bring us a drink.

The man came out with a tray with two glasses and a bottle of, well, something. It wasn't a label I recognized, but I assumed it was a wine or liquor of some sort. When he held the tray in front of me, I noticed the glass closest to me was dirty and the one closest to my host was clean. So, I reached across and picked up the clean glass. My host looked at me and chuckled. I have no idea what that was about but the drinks were then poured and I spent the next thirty minutes "milking" that single drink.

Surprisingly enough, I never felt endangered in any way, but I stayed alert to my surroundings the whole time, and maintained a friendly attitude. Everyone was cool and gracious to their new stranger.

After a while, my friend came out with the packaged painting and we were ready to go. I shook a few hands of my new friends and drinking buddies, thanked everyone and headed out the cloth door. The Jeepney was outside waiting and Mr. Hansen and I headed back into town. He dropped me off just before the bridge leading back to the base's main gate, and I walked back to the ship and to the comfort of my room. I needed to get ready and rested for leaving early in the morning.

It occurred to me a couple of times that this adventure was not one that I had really thought out. I went by myself with a man I really didn't know and rode a Jeepney out into the suburbs of a village I did not know and sat down with a group of inebriated locals who didn't know me from anyone. What came into my head was the question "What was I thinking?" I can't honestly say that I was thinking. I was naïve and trusting, and fortunately, it all turned out fine.

The haunting afterthought was that I could have disappeared forever. No one knew where I was or where I had gone. I didn't take a buddy with me, so I was on my own. If something had gone wrong and I didn't make it back to the ship, I don't know that I would have ever been able to tell this story. I would probably have been classified as AWOL, the military term for "Absent Without Leave" and charged with MSM, "Missing Ship's Movement." Since we were not in a combat zone, I wouldn't have been classified as MIA, "Missing in Action." Thank God.

The good news is I did return to the base safely with my painting carefully crated for travel. We got underway first thing the following morning and a few days later I rejoined my ship off the coast of Viet Nam and reported to duty and back on the gun line. I was happy to be back on my floating home, which eventually returned me to Yokosuka, Japan. It was an interesting story to share, but it still gives me pause when I think I was almost gone forever. That would not have been good.

By the way, all these years later, the painting still hangs in my man cave office. It fits the rest of my nautical and military décor and memorabilia, but also hangs as a reminder of an interesting and adventurous time in my life. The lesson learned when I remember how things could have turned out differently and how I was almost gone forever, does not escape me. I know I was both fortunate and blessed that somebody up in Heaven likes me and sent His angels to watch over me. I know that divine protection has happened numerous times in my life and will into the future, for however long I live. I believe it.

Navigator, where are we?

We had just left Subic Bay, the U.S. Navy's base in the Philippine Islands, south Pacific. I was the navigator aboard the USS Richard B. Anderson, a Navy destroyer. We were headed for Guam, a tiny island and base somewhere out in the middle of the Pacific Ocean. But, before we left, we had to decide the most direct route to get there in the most expedient way.

The question was do we go up and over the north end of the Philippines and then head east to Guam, or do we start west, drop south and transit east through the islands. Going up and over added another day to the trip, so the decision was to go down and through the islands.

As I recall, these were named the San Bernardino Straights and are famously known to sailors the world around, partly because they can be treacherous to navigate, and partly because of the scenic beauty they enshrine. I'm really glad the captain decided to go down and through because when we passed among the islands, and there were many, it was one of the most beautiful and calming experiences I can recall. I understand there are over one thousand islands that make up the Philippines.

As we usually did, the ship got underway early in the morning. We had quite a distance to go to clear the islands before we broke out into the Pacific Ocean on a direct route to Guam. It was going to be close but we wanted to reach the open waters before dark because we had a tight straight to pass through before clearing the islands. If possible, we preferred to do it with some daylight. The radar would certainly help us do it in the dark, but we were more concerned about all the small local fishing boats that would possibly narrow our channel of transit.

As we started east through the islands, the waters were very calm and smooth, not like glass, but very close. The sun was shining, the blue colors of the waters and the green patches of land made an incredibly beautiful and relaxing trip. As I watched from the bridge, I picked an island and fantasized about owning it, and if not living there year round, I would certainly visit a lot and bring my family and friends. What a beautiful place to be!

Late in the afternoon, based on the distance we still had to travel before dark, I spoke with the captain and he agreed to increase our speed. As we went, it still wasn't enough to get us out of the islands before dark. At one point, within hours of changing course to the east, we headed due south at twenty-five knots. It was then we began to see all the small fishing boats that spanned the horizon. Each had a light on it and there were so many boats, we could no longer tell which were village lights along the coastline, and which were on the boats. Fortunately, we had the radar to make sure we stayed close to our desired course. However, the small boats could be a problem.

The Officer of the Deck (OOD) and I discussed what we needed to do and informed the captain. He concurred. I would assume all of the responsibilities of the OOD while he was to focus all of his efforts on conning (driving) the ship and avoid hitting any of the local fishing boats. That kept him and his lookouts very busy as he wove us through the hundreds of small boats, zigging left then zigging right, back and forth for the next forty-five minutes to an hour. Even a minor collision with a local fishing boat would not reflect well on the Captain, the ship, or the US Navy, so we couldn't let that happen.

As Navigator, I still had to make sure we stayed on our course in the middle of the strait. After we'd cleared all the boats, we heaved a sigh of release. Twenty minutes later we turned east, northeast through the San Bernardino Straight and out into the Pacific Ocean. We continued on a northeast course until we reached the thirteenth parallel, then we turned to course zero nine zero and continued east toward Guam.

Back in the days following Viet Nam when most ships were still not equipped with satellite navigation and global positioning, we had to rely on the basic tools of navigating. When you're close to land, radar is very helpful to tell you where you are. If the ocean floor isn't too deep, you can use fathometer soundings to determine the depth under the ship, which is helpful to confirm about where you are. When farther away from land, we could also use LORAN, an acronym for Long Range Aids to Navigation.

Various Loran Stations are strategically placed in specific locations. One is called the master station and the second is called the slave. The master sends out a signal that triggers a response from the slave sending out overlapping signals that are spaced milliseconds apart. Loran receivers on the ship enable navigators to measure the exact millisecond overlapping lines between the two stations, confirming their location between the two stations. Tuning into the frequencies of a different pair of master and slave signals gives the navigation another millisecond line that intersects the first, pin-pointing the exact position of the ship on the surface of the ocean.

By using the lines from two or more LORAN stations, you could determine almost precisely where your ship is. However, the farther out in the ocean you are, the lines are pretty few and far between, so it's possible your true location on your chart is somewhere within five hundred to a thousand miles, which was our situation.

Using a sextant, a basic navigation tool to read the positions of the moon and stars by night and the sun by day, we could very accurately identify our location to determine if we were on course to our destination. However, in this instance we were too far from shore to use radar, the water was too deep to use soundings, and the LORAN stations were so spread out they really only served to confirm we were still in the Pacific Ocean heading east. In addition, the sky was overcast for the following three days and we had no stars at night and no sun during the day. For the navigator and his team, this created a serious challenge.

The only means of tracking our course and hoping to make our northeasterly course change to Guam was the use of a tool called Dead Reckoning. DR is a system of using the ship's course and speed, along with adjustments for wind, currents, and time since the last reliable position fix to continue to head in the determined direction to reach our destination. This was our only available tool.

As the Navigator, working with my quartermasters, I provided regular reports to the Captain as to our progress. I briefed the skipper on those tools we did not have available to us and that we were using the DR to determine our location. Although I was nervous, the Captain was fine with that and he directed me to keep him informed. I said "aye, aye" and headed back to the bridge.

My quartermasters and I were leaning over the charts, not really able to confirm exactly where we were. We tried to use all the tools to pinpoint our location, but so few were available, we could only guesstimate where we were. There was a lot of ocean between us and Guam, and at some point, we were going to need to change course thirty degrees to port in order to arrive at Guam. If we weren't close to where we thought we were, even by a couple of degrees, we could steam right past Guam without even knowing it. So, we were doing everything we could to confirm where we were, but in reality, we could only guess from the DR.

One evening, while studying the charts to try and determine our location, I heard the Officer of the Deck (OOD) call out my name and started walking over to my chart table. Keep in mind that during his watch, the OOD was entrusted with complete responsibility for the ship. Only the captain had ultimate authority and responsibility for the ship and its crew. The OOD walked over to where I was working and said, "Navigator, where are we?" Exhibiting total control and confidence, I looked down at the chart and proclaimed "Right here," as I put my finger on our best guess location on the DR track. He nodded his head, completely reassured that we were where we were supposed to be and he went back to running the ship.

I looked up at my quartermasters, smiled, tilted my head and winked. They smiled back as we bent over the charts again to try and figure out "exactly" where we were. I gave the OOD what he needed to continue his watch with confidence that everything was okay and we were on course. We were as close to where we were supposed to be as we were able to determine with the tools we had. He didn't need to worry about it because that was what I and my team were doing.

The next day right on schedule, based on our DR track and assorted calculations, we changed course thirty degrees to port and headed to where we thought Guam would be. Later that afternoon, the forward look out reported that he saw land directly ahead. I picked up my binoculars and there it was. The land was just coming over the horizon exactly "dead ahead" on the bow. It was Guam right where it was supposed to be. I called the skipper and gave him the report. We were on time and on course. He responded "Well done." I felt a sense of exhilaration and pride for my team of quartermasters. They did everything right and I heaved a sigh of relief.

If there is a lesson to be learned here, I would say it is to trust your training, trust your equipment and trust your team. I personally like to also trust in my God, my co-pilot and Supreme Navigator. After all, it is His ocean, and He always knows right where we are. Amen.

Jan and the Monkee

*"Twenty years from now, you will be more disappointed
by the things you didn't do than by the things you did – so
throw off the bowlines, sail away from the safe harbor, catch
the trade winds in your sales. Explore. Dream. Discover.*
                                                    Mark Twain

We had just arrived in Japan, and more specifically, at the US Navy base in the city of Yokosuka, just about two hours south of Tokyo. What a wonderfully new and exciting adventure this was going to be for me and my beautiful bride as we start out our marriage living in this exotic foreign land. Since I didn't yet have a home for us to move into, we settled in at the little motel located on the base, which would only be temporary until Base Housing found us a residence. The good news is that we were here together. The bad news is that two days later, I left Japan to catch my ship off the coast of Viet Nam. Okay, maybe it wasn't the best transition to our new life together, especially for her, and I realized I would have a lot to make up for later.

I'd left my wife alone, at twenty years of age, in a small motel, on a military base in a foreign country, half way around the world. Oops! If that wasn't enough, she was still on crutches from an accident she had running through a sliding glass door just a few days before we were to leave for Japan. Okay. Maybe this adventure didn't start out as we'd hoped. Regardless, we are here. Or, SHE is here.

They say it is not the challenges you run into in life, but how you deal with them, or respond to those challenges. I wouldn't know for a while how Jan was going to adjust, because I would be gone for the next two months, and she would be alone to fend for herself. I would learn later what an amazing woman I had married because she did just that, and started fending, or making the best of where she had landed. I won't tell you everything I learned when I returned home to Yokosuka, but there is one story I have to share with you. We still talk about it today.

Although Jan was young, and somewhat of a shy person, she was not one to just sit around in a motel and wait for someone to provide for her. She was also not an especially outgoing person but was rather more of an introvert up to that point. An introvert yes, but a curious one. As an officer's wife, with whatever privileges or amenities were available to her, she had heard there was a swimming pool at the Officers Club on base. So, being a southern California girl all her life, she ventured out to find the pool and see what else she could find.

When Jan entered the Club and was looking around, she heard some music coming from some place in the building. She recognized the songs and went in search of the source. As she followed the sound, walking down the comfortably carpeted hallway, she came to a set of double doors. There she could hear the music filtering out from that room. She slowly and carefully opened the door, but just enough so she could look inside to discover what was going on. Much to her delight, a rock band was rehearsing for an on-base Fourth of July concert the following day.

Still being covert to learn more, she looked around at the band and noticed the lead singer, who was discussing the number they were working on. When he turned around, Jan realized it was actually him. It was the real Davy Jones of the world famous, "Hey, hey, we're the Monkees", Monkees rock band.

Right there, on the other side of the world from home, within thirty feet, was her favorite rock group, and the adorable Davy Jones, her teenage heart throb. It took every restraint she could muster not to scream out loud and rush the band. Instead, she closed the door and returned to the motel to retrieve her camera and hurry back to the O'Club, hopefully in time to maybe, possibly, get a picture. "Please, please, please."

This time, with a little more boldness, Jan slipped into the small meeting room and settled just inside the door and started taking photos with her Kodak Instamatic Camera. Suddenly, she became aware of a rather big man walking in her direction.

Uh, ohh! He was large enough that she realized he was either security or a bodyguard for the band. Now, she began to get nervous about being there and became anxious for what she feared was about to happen. When the guard approached her, he asked her who she was and what she was doing there. When she told me this story later, her response took me very much by surprise. Jan stood up and blurted out, "I'm a photographer from the Stars and Stripes newspaper, and I am here to get photos of Davy Jones and the band for an article about the upcoming concert," or something to that effect, as best I can recall how the story was told to me.

I had to laugh in amazement at her quick thinking, but we both knew that was a lie. A lie? My innocent, young wife just told a lie? I didn't know that was even possible. However, the security guy seemed satisfied and turned around to walk back to his duty station near the band.

Jan was heaving a sigh of relief and was settling in to enjoy the rest of the rehearsal, when half way there, the gentleman stopped, turned around, and headed back in Jan's direction. Uh ohh, again. Busted!

Now she was in trouble, with no escape. As he approached, he asked: "Don't professional news photographers use thirty-five millimeter cameras?" Jan's face went blank as she stuttered out, "a what?" She knew she was caught and began a very quiet, humble and sincere barrage of explanation in the form of an apology. "I am so sorry" she repeated over and over as he stopped in front of her, arms crossed and physically imposing. "I love the Monkees and have always been a fan, and my favorite has always been Davy Jones. I'm sorry. I just wanted to hear the music and watch the rehearsal." Apparently, her efforts, charm, meekness and beauty softened the guard who chuckled, smiled and said she could stay if she would sit down and not make any noise. She does have charm and a magic about her that way. It always worked on me. Jan didn't need any more encouragement to be completely submissive and comply with his instructions.

The story continues.

At the end of the rehearsal, the kind man came back and told Jan that Davy wanted to meet her. So, he escorted her across the room and she had a brief "meet and greet" with this amazing superstar. Davy was so accommodating and welcoming and prompted Jan to hand her camera to the guard so he could take a few pictures of her with Davy. He even put his arm around her and snuggled her in close.

Was this a dream come true, or what? Since Mr. Jones was supposed to have dinner with the base Commander and his daughter that evening, I believe he was hoping Jan was the Admiral's daughter. Unfortunately for him, she wasn't. When the Admiral finally arrived with his twelve-year-old daughter, I'm guessing Davy was also a little disappointed. I suspect Jan was also disappointed she wasn't invited to join them.

The story continues.

As Jan thanked Mr. Jones and was saying good bye, he surprised her once more with some very special instructions. He asked her if she was coming to the show the next day and she excitedly confirmed that she was. So, in his kindness, he instructed her that when she came to the concert, a bit early, she should go to the stairs at the left side of the stage and meet up with his security guard, and that he would have a seat for her.

On the Fourth of July, 1972, on the Navy base in Yokosuka, Japan, Jan arrived early and found the security guard waiting for her at the stairs, as instructed. He escorted her over to the front row to a reserved VIP seat, immediately in front of the center stage. During the "concert of a lifetime," she fired off the remaining photos of her now infamous, Kodak Instamatic camera. I was very happy for her, and to this day, I am grateful to Davy Jones and an unnamed security guard for their kindness. For her, it was one of the most memorable experiences of her life, up to that point, and a great start to her new adventure in a foreign land, so far, far from home. After hearing the memorable and exciting story upon my return back to Yokosuka, I thought to myself, "I don't need to worry about her. She will be okay."

The story continues.

Almost forty years later, as Jan and I were coming up on our anniversary, our children surprised us with tickets to a Monkees concert at the beautiful Clark County Amphitheatre here in Washington state just north of Vancouver. I contacted the local newspaper, The Columbian, and spoke to a reporter I had worked with before. He was very interested in telling the story. We provided him the pictures Jan had taken back in Yokosuka, Japan, both during the rehearsal, and the following day during the actual concert on the base. We were also able to make arrangements, with great effort, and met Davy Jones and Peter Tork during the "meet and greet" following the concert.

Since Jan took eight by ten inch copies of the photos from almost forty years ago, Davy Jones was very gracious and autographed them. He even appeared to remember the encounter. In the original photo, Davy was wearing a green and white, thick striped jacket, and Jan was wearing a flowery pink blouse. When he was looking at the photo, he said: "I still have that jacket." Jan responded: "I still have that blouse." At that point, I think it all clicked.

The Greater Sin

*"You cannot escape the responsibility of tomorrow by
evading it today."*

Abraham Lincoln

I was ten years old and living in San Francisco, California, where my parents were going through seminary to become ordained ministers. Maybe that is ironic considering the story I'm about to tell you. You know what they say about "preacher's kids." Who, me?

Sometimes, my brothers and I must have had too much time on our hands. That is probably not too different than what a lot of boys experience in their ages ranging from eight to eleven. In our constant search for adventures and entertainment, we sometimes found ourselves getting involved or doing something we wouldn't otherwise have done if we'd really thought it through or had the foresight to see the consequences.

Before my parents were accepted into the ministry and our family moved to San Francisco for their training, we spent most of our young lives growing up on a farm. We'd learned to be somewhat self-sufficient in the great outdoors experiencing everything nature had to share with us, including cuts, scrapes, stings, bites, and even poison oak in our private body areas. We climbed trees of all shapes and sizes from the massively huge oak tree we referred to as the "monkey tree", to eighty-foot-high Eucalyptus trees, as well as apple and cherry trees. We were fearless in those days. If I saw my kids today climbing some of the trees we climbed when I was a kid, I would be horrified and probably put down some pretty fast and hard rules.

We also dug underground forts at the end of long underground tunnels.

During hay season, we made massive above ground forts and tunnels from the bales of hay when the farmer finished a field. He was grateful that we did the work of accumulating all the bales in one spot when he came out to pick them up. On a few occasions, we tested our carpentry skills by constructing tree houses, forts in the air. I think we tried to do it all. Each project gave us purpose, and there is no distance too far, an adventure too dangerous for us to attempt, or resources too few for us to complete a project. When we didn't have exactly what we needed, we got really creative and improvised.

Living out in the country, we were pretty free to go just about anywhere we wanted and do almost anything we wanted. We rode horses, herded cattle and slopped pigs. We also got involved in a number of farm activities on the three-hundred-and-sixty-acre property, including bailing hay, cleaning barn stalls, raising cows, rabbits, pigs and a lot more. Some of our adventures included hunting, although we were somewhat limited in the size of our prey by our only approved choice of weapons. Once we got over the thrills and limitations of self-made slingshots, we eventually moved on to Bee-Bee guns, and our range and accuracy increased quite a bit. In order to keep our Bee-Bee guns, we had to promise to be smart and safe in our use of them.

For the most part, we were very safe with only an occasionally miss-directed shot into a window or other forbidden targets. We actually became very proficient in our skills and could hit most targets consistently. That's fine out in the rural country. However, when moving to the city, there are a whole new set of rules and expectations in using firearms, even an air-powered Bee-Bee gun rifle.

The seminary where my parents were training in San Francisco pretty much covered a full city block. It was an attractive and well-maintained facility and kept clean by the cadets going through the training. Cleaning was just one of their many responsibilities in addition to various classes. Along the second story walkway, there was metal railing filled in by wired glass panels. They were textured glass, so they weren't very clear, but the wire woven through them gave them a considerable level of strength and durability providing safety for those walking along the outside covered walkways.

I got curious one day, and therein lay the temptation and subsequent poor choice. It must have been my scientific interest that made me want to test a theory. I acknowledge that what I am about to tell you is a confession from the sins of a ten-year-old. I'm just hoping that the statute of limitations has run out on this particular crime.

Remember the Bee-Bee guns I grew up with? Well, I decided to see if the glass panels were strong enough to withstand the impact of a BB launched from a BB-gun air rifle. So, when no one was around, except an un-named brother and friend, I took aim and fired into the lower right-hand corner of one of the glass panels.

Unfortunately, my accuracy was still good. Fortunately, the impact of the BB wasn't powerful enough to break out the glass. Unfortunately, it was powerful enough to make a very distinctive hole in the glass, which clearly could only be made by a BB gun, which my dad knew I had. If anyone was to discover the hole and it was determined that it came from a BB gun, I'm pretty certain the culprit would very quickly be identified as me. That was not good. Now, I had to make a decision. Was I going to have to "fess up", which meant confess my sin, or was I going to be creative enough to deflect the attention in some other direction. In all honesty, today, I hope that my mind wasn't that diabolical. I prefer to think I was resourceful with a strong sense of self-preservation.

An idea came to me almost instantly when I saw a little red wagon sitting nearby. I don't think I thought much about it, but just took action to cover my poor choice of targets. I rolled the wagon over to the glass panel where I had shot and made the hole. The tongue of the handle happened to be at the exact height of the BB hole in the glass. I folded the handle back so the tongue provided the leading edge of my substitute battering ram, backed up a few feet, and rolled the wagon into the glass. The wire held, and I didn't crash through the railing to the parking area below, but the crash caused enough damage to the glass that the BB hole was completely obscured. I left the wagon there and went and put my BB gun away.

The BB hole was the first sin, and the wagon cover-up was the greater sin. I stayed away from that area for quite some time before venturing back to see if it had been discovered. If I had been questioned, regardless of what I would say, I'm sure my guilty expression and red face would have given me away.

Nothing was ever said about it. I don't even know if someone tried to find out or just decided that an accident had occurred and no one was going to "fess up." Not too long after that, the panel had been replaced and life went on. I didn't do that again, ever. Am I sorry? Yes, definitely. Even to this date, and during this writing, I still feel a certain level of guilt and shame for having shot the glass, but even more for my efforts to cover it up.

I seriously don't think I'm going to Hell for having shot the BB into the glass at age ten, or for breaking out the glass in attempt to cover it up, and then actually getting away with it. Boys will be boys, but that is certainly not a justification for my actions.

Over the years, including with my own children, my nieces and nephews, and my grandchildren, I often wonder what curiosity it is that makes children do some of the things they do. I can't even answer that question, but what does come to mind is a line from a popular country western song that says: "What was I thinking?" I don't even have a good answer. However, if my dad had found out, he would have asked me that question. I'd have probably said "I don't know," and then, he would have given me something to think about.

I doubt if I'm the only person who has ever done things, dumb things, that I would later regret having done, especially where there was damage or hurt involved. Hopefully, those have been kept to a minimum over the years and I've grown up with a greater appreciation for life, property and doing the right thing.

I believe I have. I also hope that I have done more good by a hundred-fold than those things I shouldn't have, not as a means of atonement because I've already been forgiven, but I believe we all want to do good and make a difference. We want to get to the end of life and be able to look back and believe we have made a difference and that mankind is better off for us having lived. I've heard it said that "I can't do everything, but I can do something." I hope I'm making a difference in my part of the world as a result of lessons learned.

Hit the Deck
My side is trying to kill me

"Learning is not compulsory – neither is survival."
W. Edward Deming

It was nearing the end of the Viet Nam war, and we were on patrol in the south China seas. My ship was traveling in formation with seven other ships, escorting the USS Hancock, CVW-21, one of our countries magnificent naval aircraft carriers. This is not unusual at all to have a number of ships providing escort services for one of our carriers. That is the way it is. The destroyers, cruisers and assorted other ships provide support and protection for these magnificent "cities in a can."

You might imagine that with all that massive firepower, a carrier should be pretty secure on their own. That is true. However, a carrier is also quite large, one thousand feet or more in length, which restricts it's maneuverability to some degree. Un-escorted, a carrier could be an easy target for submarines. The escorts, especially the smaller destroyers and cruisers, are much more maneuverable and provide a perimeter of security and protection for these significant floating communities. When I see one, the word "impressive" always comes to mind.

These massive carriers are like small cities with over forty-five hundred crew members onboard to operate every aspect of this community, including maintaining the equipment, providing electricity, water, food and just about anything else you'd find in a small town. Then, because the aircraft carrier's primary purpose is to have a platform that will serve as a base for the aircraft it carries, you also then need to add the twenty-seven hundred members of the air wing that services and maintains the aircraft, along with the flight crews, you now have a small city of almost seven thousand men. The carrier also stores the various bombs, bullets, rockets and assorted armament for use by its planes.

My ship was the USS Richard B. Anderson, DD-786, one of the smaller escort vessels. The USS Anderson was a veteran of World War II and measured three hundred and ninety feet from stem to stern. For those not familiar with nautical terms, the stem is the pointy end at the front of the ship and the stern is the butt end at the very back of the ship. The pointy end is also called the bow of the ship.

As an escort ship, the Anderson was pretty quick with a top speed of thirty-six knots and was very maneuverable. With the double rudders and twin screws (propellers), we had learned how to configure both at any given moment to turn on a dime (ok, maybe a silver dollar) and immediately head in a new direction if called for.

The Anderson had some modifications made to it since WWII and now had two five-inch thirty-eight gun mounts located on the forward part of the ship. This was just in front of the "bridge", which is the space from which we drove the ship. Located thirty-six feet above the waterline with lots of windows, the bridge gave us great visibility in all directions forward. When we stepped out of the bridge onto the "wings" of the bridge, we could look aft (toward the back) and see just about anything behind us, even something directly behind us in the distance.

It was a beautiful, sunny day with calm seas when we received a radio message from the formation commander aboard the USS Hancock. The only thing I could figure is that the aircraft carrier we were escorting was either bored or needed to off-load some of the tons of ammunition they were carrying. We were directed to form a single file line directly behind the carrier. They said they were going to give us a show. We didn't know what to expect, but we quickly fell into our place in the formation behind the carrier. The Anderson was a junior ship so we were positioned further back in the line. It didn't really matter, though, since we all had a great position from which to watch the impressive display of fire power.

I was done with my bridge watch at the time, so I changed into some shorts and sandals and found my spot on the flight deck which was aft of the mid-section, where I thought to be the best place for viewing the show. I wasn't on duty, along with quite a few of the crew, so I decided I would lie out on the flight deck, watch the show and catch some sun rays on my body. It was a lazy afternoon in West Pac and I was ready for some relaxation.

Once the show started, it consisted of a number of alternating fly-bys from the Hancock air wing that flew down the port side of the line of ships at about two thousand yards, equal to about one nautical mile. Some planes used their machine gun cannons to strafe the water, and we could see spouts and sprays of water launching skyward as the bullets impacted the surface. Other planes dropped bombs that created very impressive plumes and mushrooms of water as they impacted the surface and exploded. It really was an impressive show.

At one point, a jet made his run and dropped his bomb, but this time it was different and got a whole lot more exciting. There were about thirty of us sitting around the small helicopter flight deck when the bomb hit the water and exploded. Suddenly, we could all see small plumes of water bursting above the surface and headed in a straight path for our ship. There was very little reaction time, maybe five to eight seconds, but we all figured out what was happening at the same time. There was a piece of shrapnel from the bomb that had just exploded and it was skipping across the water directly in line with the flight deck of the Anderson. We all scattered and quite a few of us dove into the covered helicopter hangar next to the flight deck. We weren't looking back but were scrambling and piling on each other in the nearby protection. After a couple of seconds, I jumped up and ran out to see if it had skipped over the ship. It was still skipping on the starboard side and away from the ship. That was close.

Best we could figure, it skipped directly over the flight deck at about two to three feet. Someone could have been hurt or killed if they had stayed on the flight deck and not run for cover. That gave us something to talk about for the next couple of weeks as well as something to write home about. It was the most exciting and memorable part of the day. The show finished and we all formed up in our normal escort formation and sailed on to our next mission assignment.

No one was hurt, thankfully and if somebody had been injured or killed, it would have been an accident classified as injury or death by "friendly fire."

Prior to this experience, I'd spent a year and a half along with many of my shipmates running missions off the coast of Viet Nam, including some close-in fire missions north of the DMZ. During those missions, we counted ninety-six incoming enemy rounds, some landing very close to the ship, but never hitting us. Even with our gunfire support missions, we were occasionally close enough to see a lot of action on the beach and beyond. However, the experience of the fly-by strafing and bombing show was the first time I'd really felt that I was in serious danger of being injured or killed. Adrenaline was high and I could hear the nervous laughter and joking that followed all around me. At one point, I said to my buddy, "What did I do? I think my side is trying to kill me." We joked and laughed that nervous laughter for the next twenty minutes, and then went about our duties as usual, just another day serving our county. Thank God! All's well that ends well.

Did I ever tell you the story?

"Discover, develop and apply your talents, for they are gifts to be used in service to you and others."
Eric Allenbaugh

One of the absolute greatest joys of life is having children, and that is certainly true for me. I am even blessed to have three children, all boys except two girls. My first child was a beautiful girl and perfect in every way. Twenty months later, Jan and I had our second girl who is just as beautiful and perfect in every way. It was a little over nine years before we were blessed with a son, and a very special one in so many ways.

I have to admit, and I am thankful, they all certainly got their good looks from their mom, that's for sure. At another time I will tell you the story of each of these children, now all grown-up and each one unique in their own way. They have taught me so many things about being a father, leading a family, raising children, and that it is possible for our children to be our friends as well with family always being first.

One of the things I tried to do was to make the most of our outings by creating an adventure or fun in some way, even while traveling to church. So, one of the things I used to do to help pass the time was to tell stories. I very rarely recited the traditional stories because the girls had already heard most of them in their younger years.

Back before my son James was born, we lived in the Anaheim, California area and had to travel about forty minutes to get to our church in Santa Ana. It usually took so long, not because of the distance, but because of the freeway traffic and the number of city streets we had to travel. Sunday was one thing, but during the week after being at school all day, the kids had little interest or enthusiasm in traveling down to the church for mid-week activities and rehearsals.

On one particular Wednesday evening, we were headed to our music rehearsal, but Jan wasn't able to go. It was just me, Kristie and Kelly. I would always start out by asking "Did I ever tell you the story of…" and then would throw in a topic of some sort. The girls would answer "no." and I would start building the story as we went along. It was spontaneous, challenging and a lot of fun.

On one trip I asked them "Did I ever tell you the story of Chocolate Mountain?" They responded "no," and then I began. The story was about two little girls by the names of Kristie and Kelly who were sisters who had started out one day on a walk. Along the way, they discovered a mountain that was all chocolate, with trees and bushes sprinkled with just about every type of candy imaginable. I had no idea what would happen next until that point in the story and it just kept going. It was a story with no end, at least until we arrived at our destination. They'd ask what happened next and I'd assure them we would finish the story on the way home.

By the end of the choir and band rehearsals, I'd forgotten all about the story. It didn't matter because once we got in the car to head home, one or both of the girls would say "Tell us about Chocolate Mountain, dad. Finish the story." So off we went, discovering cookies, candy cane fences, caramel caves, licorice sticks, rock candies, and we even located a couple of cotton candy bushes. It was fun to listen to the girls react, laugh and engage in the stories, which urged me on to continue until we were almost home. I always found a way to wrap it up before arriving in our carport. The girls rushed in the house to share the story with their mom. I had such a great time.

Vacations were a little more challenging because we could be in the car for anywhere from eight to twelve hours or more depending on where we were headed. One year, my older brother who was in medical school in Salt Lake City, was getting married and all the family was coming from everywhere to be there. We were still living in Anaheim so it was a considerable trip with the four of us in the car. My wife, Jan, and I decided to make the trip a big adventure stopping at various sites, including Las Vegas and a couple of national parks on the way there. But, on the way home, there wasn't as much to see except we now had our sights set on taking the girls to the Grand Canyon.

It was a long trip again, but a beautiful drive through Utah and then down into Arizona. The landscape was fascinating to me with all the desert colors, plateaus, and gigantic rock formations that went on as far as the eyes could see.

As I saw a specific rock formation, my imagination went to work and I saw something in my mind that may not really have been there, but it was close enough to start a story. I'd ask "Did I ever tell you the story of…..," then, I'd pause for a moment until I had the girls' attention, and I would add something like "the sleeping Indian princess?" They would answer "no" and I would be off and running with whatever came to mind. On this day, there was a large plateau that looked like it could have been a woman lying on her back with all the obvious peaks, curves and projections. I can't give you the whole story in these few pages, but the story was about a young Indian maiden who was in love with a handsome brave. She was the daughter of the Chief, and the Indian brave had to prove his love for her through courage in a great battle or major hunts for the tribe. He was indeed courageous and he and the maiden were going to be married. However, the brave went off to a fierce battle and was never to return. This saddened the maiden to the point where she could no longer live without her brave. She went up to the mountain top and lay down on her back asking the great spirits to bring her Brave back to her. She would sleep there until he returned. He never did and to this day, the beautiful Indian maiden still lays there on the high mountain plateau waiting for her love to return.

That was just one story, but the girls were intrigued and wanted to hear more. I told them I would tell them another story as soon as I saw a sign that reminded me of that particular, yet-to- be-created story. The focus of each story was subject to the various rock formations as they appeared out ahead.

There was <u>The Lost Pony</u>, the <u>Spirit Bear</u>, the <u>Guardian Eagle</u>, the <u>Hidden Magic Fountain</u> and more, but I don't remember them all. The desert formations provided the inspiration for each story and made the trip go a lot faster, for me as well as the girls. I think Jan was even entertained. It got to the point where all I had to do was ask the question, "Did I ever tell you the story ……" and before I could even announce the subject, Kristie, Kelly and Jan would say "Oh, right. There he goes again." Then they would all laugh and give me that special look. Does that mean they didn't believe me?

It was great fun for me and it provided some entertainment throughout the trip, and my girls will reference back to the time we made the trip to the Grand Canyon. After my son was born and a few years older, the girls asked me to tell Jimmy about some of the stories they remembered. Then they'd say, "Oh here he goes again," followed by laughter. That was ok with me. It's a fun memory that I will cherish forever. Who knows, I may even be called on to share those stories with my grandchildren. When I am, I'm good to go. There's always more where that came from. By the way, "Did I ever tell you the story about…..?"

One Day

"Success isn't permanent and failure isn't terminal."
Mike Ditka

Being somewhat of an entrepreneur, I was introduced to a network marketing company that provides essential services to their customers. It was different than anything else I had ever gotten involved in.

Yes, like so many others, it is a multi-level marketing company that provides an opportunity to initially generate some additional income. Over time, it could also generate residual income that could eventually become a person's <u>primary</u> source of income. Since it is residual, that means the income check continues to arrive week after week, month after month, and even year after year, even though the work was done just one time. As long as a customer is using the essential services, which everyone is going to do from now until forever, you continue to receive a small residual from each payment made for those services. The key, though, is that the independent business owner must be willing to follow the plan and do the work.

This is very much like insurance companies where the agent receives a small residual income each time their customer makes their monthly premium payment. Or, it's like the royalties that come to artists for their one-time work, whether it's composing, writing or performing. Consider the amount of income that is continually generated by Elvis Presley's legacy through his music sales. His family continues to enjoy the benefits of the work he accomplished during his, unfortunately, short life. But, his work keeps on giving.

This network marketing business made so much sense to me that I got started and began following the plan. That includes attending regular training sessions to learn more about the products and services of the business, observe the process of presenting the business to others who would like to change their life and secure their future, learn to be a leader like the friends that introduced me to the business, and to provide leadership to those in my down line organization. It's a proven plan, so the smartest thing I could do was to follow the plan and not try to re-invent it.

This company is so on top of it; they totally understand the need to award progress and to acknowledge success to individual and team efforts in front of their peers. So, this is done pretty much on a weekly basis.

The recognition time is both encouraging to the individuals receiving recognition, but also to those who are watching the presentation because it inspires them to want to succeed and also get acknowledged. People may say that they either don't need the recognition, or they don't like attention being brought to them. I've also learned over the years that people really do need, and even hunger to be acknowledged and valued, and this company does it extremely well, even for the small steps.

A lot of people work for years at their jobs, but never receive any kind of personal acknowledgement, recognition or reward. Unlike this company, I didn't see much in other companies I worked for, even when we set records or developed new programs for which the company benefited. How about you? I guess the rationale in these other company's thinking was that the work is what we get paid for and that we are just doing our job. Unfortunately, for most people with a "job", that is the reality of what can be expected.

In my opinion, it is the network marketing companies that do the best job of rewarding and acknowledging success and achievement. It certainly is the case with the company I am involved in. Each week during the training sessions, usually near the end of the meeting, there is a period of recognition. They always start at the smallest levels of achievement, although each achievement is treated like it is the most important step that the individual has taken, which it is at the time. It means they are moving forward and having success, and they are ready to strive toward their new goal, the next level.

Remember, long term success begins with baby steps, followed by continual and consistent effort to achieve higher levels. A big achievement is just the accumulation of a bunch of small daily, weekly and monthly achievements. If you need a visual, I liken it to the time I saw a jet fly by my aircraft carrier and broke the sound barrier. I could see him coming, but there was little sound building until he passed us, at which time there was a huge explosion when all of the sound reached us at the same moment. It was very impressive. We felt the explosion almost as much as we heard it. "VerrrBOOOOOOMMMmm!" A bunch of littles makes a lot.

At one specific Saturday training, I was called up to the front of the room, along with a few other people who had achieved the level of ETL (Executive Team Leader), my third promotion in a few months since becoming an Independent Business Owner with my network marketing company. Sometimes, the leader of the award presentations will stop one or two of the recipients to ask them a couple of questions, like who they are, what their occupation has been, and then, "How long did it take you to achieve ETL?" Over the months I've heard responses for achieving various levels anywhere from a couple of days, weeks, or months, and with the highest levels of leadership and organizations, it could be a few years.

When the leader asked me that same question, my response was simple and surprising. He asked me how long it took me to reach ETL, and my response was "One day." I think that shocked him, and even caught him off guard. So, he asked me to clarify by questioning, "One day?" Again, I said "Yes", and then I went on to explain. "One day I wasn't an ETL, and the next day, I was." Initially, I think everyone was surprised, but after my brief explanation, everyone seemed to understand and laughed along with the leader and me. No one achieves ETL in one day, although with the right circumstances, I think it is perfectly feasible.

In reality, at the time, I had been involved in the business for a little over four months, so I suppose the correct answer should have been "a little over four months." But the point I was making, was more about that I had achieved that level, than it was that it took me a little over four months to get there.

I believe it is more important for each person to achieve their goals at their ability and desire for the position, even if it is slow and steady, rather than it was equal to, greater or less than it took anyone else. I personally love the challenge that comes to me when so-and-so did it in a certain number of days or months. It gives me a goal to shoot for and challenges me to do it faster.

However, it is not like that for many people. For some people, circumstances and abilities are different, and they may decide they can't do it in the same time frame as someone else, so they stop trying, or even quit because they believe they can't do it as fast or as grandiose as somebody else. That unfortunate mindset may hurt someone else's journey and may even prevent them from continuing.

I don't want to be the cause of them making that life-changing decision. I would rather that everyone takes "one day" at a time and keep moving forward to achieve the end goal whatever that is for that person. As I've said to my team, "do one thing every day for your business." Rather than working at it occasionally, maybe even in unscheduled bursts, we should do at least one thing every day to move us closer to our goal and achieve success. Consistency is the key. That creates momentum. I believe it also provides a greater incentive for us to keep going, working with our leadership and being a leader by setting the example.

One other point I'd like to make. Although it may be subtle at first, I believe it is not only important, but can be significant. It's the difference between saying "one day" or "some day."

Using the words "one day" implies that it <u>is</u> going to happen and that it is a definite. The problem with saying "some day," is that it is too open-ended, giving a person an "out" or excuse, which means it may never happen. There isn't enough personal commitment to "some day" statements. What we do know for sure is that "life happens" and there are many things that get in the way because we are not always in control of everything that happens to us. People become ill, some people get laid off or lose their job altogether. Many people get married, and some get divorced. However, we can choose how we will react and deal with each of those occurrences, and "one day" says to me that a person is still in the game. It is still their goal, and "one day", I will achieve my goal of financial independence.

Tuck this in the back of your mind and get back to me in a couple of years. One day, one of the founders or senior executives of my company is going to ask me how long it took me to achieve SVP (Senior Vice President)." My response will still be, "one day."

My Wife for Life

*"It's not the partner's job to be more loveable. It's your job
to be more loving."*

Barbara DeAngelis

The first time I saw her was at a summer music camp in the canyons of Malibu, California. We didn't go to the same church, but our churches were of the same denomination. So, all of the kids from eight to eighteen years of age from the southern California division of our church, went to the same summer music program each year.

The music camp was for ten days at a beautiful and secluded place called Mountain Crags Camp, located in the hills of Malibu Canyon. It was a great place for a wonderful music learning experience as well as to meet friends that we would see for years to come. Band camp was where everyone wanted to go and the camp was the place where we all wanted to work during our summer breaks.

Her name was Janet and she was undoubtedly the cutest girl at the camp, and I wanted to meet her. I was twelve at the time and Janet was nine years old. So, I walked up and asked if she would go with me on the moonlight hike, one of the special traditions and highlights during the two weeks of music camp. However, she said, "No!" I said "Nuts to you" and walked back to my friends who were watching in amusement. Hmmm? That was that, at least for now.

I would see Janet every year at the same camp, but I was no longer interested in her, or that is at least what I told myself. I kept up the image, although subconsciously, for many years.

I didn't know it at the time, but when she turned fourteen, she decided she was going to marry me. At sixteen, the prospect of marriage was not even in my head as a conscious thought. But, not too long after that she asked me out on our first date to a church banquet for the music departments of her church. I took two weeks to decide to accept the invitation and go. I had a number of friends that would be there as well. I was still playing semi-interested in Jan.

Over the next couple of years, Janet was persistent, and I began to take serious notice of her and our relationship grew. I started calling her Jan instead of Janet. I really don't think I was a slow learner, but rather slow to make a serious commitment to anyone.

One evening, Jan and I had a serious disagreement, although I can't tell you what that was about. I was leaving her house and was headed home when she followed me out to the car. She was in tears and asked me not to go. Then she asked if she would ever see me again? I don't know what came over me, but I blurted out, "Yes, I love you too much", then I added "stupid." She said "what did you say?", and I just drove off.

I guess that was the point when I knew I was in love with her and wanted to spend the rest of my life with her. That is a whole other story for another time. It was a couple of years before she asked me to marry her. Yes, you heard me right. She asked me, although she later said she was just kidding.

Just before I was commissioned as an officer from the Navy Officer Candidate School in Newport, RI, Jan came out from California to visit and attend my commissioning. It was then I asked her to marry me, and fortunately she said yes.

After I was commissioned and completed Surface Warfare School, I was assigned to a Navy destroyer in Yokosuka, Japan where I would be home ported. I returned to the states in mid-March of that year for an engineering school in San Diego, CA, so we moved our wedding up and were married on April 8, 1972. Thus, began our life together.

When we recited our vows during our wedding ceremony, we made them for life. It is true that we had some difficult periods over the years as I believe most marriages do. However, we always worked through them together and grew as a couple. It never occurred to me or Jan that it was supposed to be any other way.

Jan was my wife for life, and that was all I knew, and it has proven to have been the best commitment I have ever made. I am grateful to her for deciding at age fourteen that she was going to marry me. It took me a while longer to smarten up and come around to her way of thinking. There were temptations and opportunities over the years, but I knew I had too much to lose to yield to any of those temptations. Today I can't imagine spending my life with anyone else. There could be no better life partner for me, and I'd do anything for her.

Not too many years ago, I went to a men's retreat in northern Oregon, about an hour from our home in Vancouver, WA. It was a beautiful and rustic location and it gave me a chance to get to know many of the men from the church in an attempt to be more involved. We had meetings and events throughout the day, ending each evening with a message from our guest speaker followed by a fellowship time. After refreshments, we all returned to our cabins for a follow-up discussion on the subject of the evening message. On this one particular night, it had to do with marriage.

There were about seven men in my cabin, and one was assigned by the retreat committee as our cabin leader for the follow-up discussions. Our leader told his story about his marriage and divorce to his wife, with whom he had since re-married. However, they were considering divorcing again. As we went around the room, the other men, ages ranging from twenty years to the mid sixties, were either recently divorced, considering divorce, or with one young man, he was engaged for the past six months but wasn't sure it was going to work out.

Everyone had a chance to share what was going on in their life and marriage, and how the message from the speaker was relevant to their situation. I was pretty quiet, and up to that point hadn't said a word, just listened. The leader finally turned to me and pointed out that they hadn't heard from me. I hadn't responded because Jan and I had been married for just over thirty-four years at that point. I was happily married and had no thoughts that it would be any other way.

I knew I had to choose my words very carefully before I spoke, but I also had to be honest in my response. These men were having issues and struggling to varying degrees with their marriages or engagement. My heart ached for them and I didn't want to come across either uncaring or self-righteous in any way. Jan and I have had our issues over the years, but we always worked through them. We believed in the old adage of never going to bed angry, and for the most part, we never did. Making up was always the best part.

When I finally spoke, I told them a little about my background and my life with Jan. I told them we'd met when she was nine and I was twelve. I shared a little about our life together, where we had lived and some of the challenges we had faced. In finishing my response, for whatever it is worth, I wanted to at least leave them with something to think about.

I shared with them that when they are thinking about their marriage and the person they swapped vows with, I recommended they think back and recall the reasons they fell in love in the first place, and more importantly, what were the reasons that made them decide to get married and start out on a life together. I suggested they consider thinking back to when their mind was so pre-occupied with wanting to be with her and spend so much time with her that is all they could think about.

Everything was about being together, and at the time, nothing else was more important. We would change our schedule or even stand up some friends if there was a chance to spend time with that special person. It's good to think about the promises made to love, honor and cherish her "till death do you part." As that question runs though your head, ask yourself, "did you really mean it?" And if you did, take the time to think about and look at it again. You probably have a lot invested in the relationship already, emotionally, physically and spiritually.

No one challenged me. They were all gracious enough to hear me out. I hope it did give them something to think about and maybe it helped at least one of them. I can only speak my belief and offer my input. After all, they asked. I can't control if they heard it, understood it, or acted on it. It's up to them.

One of the truths that I live with, as does everyone else, is that I never know the time or day when I may no longer be on this earth. To that point, one of my all-time favorite country entertainers is Garth Brooks. In 1989, he came out with a song that expresses exactly what I feel every day as it relates to my relationship with Jan and others I care so much about. It's called "If Tomorrow Never Comes," and the chorus nails it for me. He sings:

"If tomorrow never comes, will she know how much I loved her?
Did I try in every way, to show her every day, that she's my only one.
And if my time on earth were through, and she
must face this world without me,
Is the love I gave her in the past, gonna be enough to last,
If tomorrow never comes.
So, tell that someone that you love, just what you're thinking of,
If tomorrow never comes."

Over the years, I have been tempted, and there have been opportunities to be with other women. Fortunately, I never pursued it or allowed it to go forward, but at those rare and most tempting times for me, I remembered how much I would lose and what the cost would be if I'd ever betrayed Jan. I couldn't do it. She is seriously the "best" thing that has ever happened to me and I can't imagine it any other way.

I'm in no hurry to reach my fiftieth or sixtieth anniversary. They will get here soon enough. But when I do, I will celebrate them and all those anniversaries in between with Janet, because as I promised, she is my wife for life.

I Love Julia Roberts

Truth is always the strongest argument."

Sophocles

I don't think it is a big stretch to assume that almost everyone who has ever spent time in a theater or in front of a television has developed an appreciation for a favorite actor or two, whether male or female. Some men fall in love with a female character and are drawn to her in some magical or fantasy way. I certainly have and could spend a great deal of time telling you about all my favorite performers, male and female. The males are usually the "hero" types with strengths that I want to see in me. The females are the ones that I want to save and take care of in some way.

Skilled actors have the ability to take a role and bring that character to life in such a way that you are completely absorbed into the story line and develop a relationship with that character. It's not realistic, but it does provide a place to escape to, even if only for short periods of time. These respites into the world of make believe provide time to get away, to escape, to regroup mentally, and sometimes gain the encouragement needed to deal with the challenges of every day living. These fantasy adventures are many times in contrast to our own lives and give us a change from our day to day routines

This is a perfectly normal and entertaining way to keep us healthy and exercise our imaginations. Like anything in moderation, this is probably a good thing. A story and a character may hit us the strongest at a time when we may need to feel some specific emotion, so we relate in a way that makes most sense at the time.

I believe that my wife's all time favorite male actor is Tom Selleck.

We've all enjoyed his characters over the years, but I know that Jan is drawn to his good looks for sure, his cuteness and whimsical smile, from the days of Magnum P.I. Her cell phone ring is the theme from the Magnum PI television show. One day, my wife told me that if Tom Selleck ever called her, she was out the door. I asked her if she had his phone number so I could call him and let him know. She was joking, I'm sure, and so was I. However, I don't know that I would ever make that call if I was so inclined. Jan is an incredibly and naturally beautiful, strong and intelligent woman, and if Mr. Selleck knew how incredible she is, he might make the call himself. I don't want to take that chance.

Over the years, Jan's also developed a fondness for other good-looking performers like Shawn Cassidy, Robert Redford, Christopher Reeves, and most recently, Johnny Depp. I can't argue that she certainly has good taste. She fell in love with Robert Redford a long time ago when she saw him in his white Navy service dress uniform in the movie, "The Way We Were." I've never been as good looking as Robert Redford, but she related that image to me in my identical navy white uniform when I was a young Naval officer during the Viet Nam war. My hair was also blond and combed in the same way as Redford in that movie. I'm the lucky guy.

For most people, these kinds of fantasies from afar are harmless and normal, and healthy people enjoy the idea, but are mostly content in their own life and relationships. Jan and I certainly are, and the occasional bantering back and forth is a fun game we play. Fortunately, our lives are full and we don't have the time or the inclination to run away with these fictional characters. If we did, in reality, I'm sure we'd be disappointed.

Now, going back to my original thought where I had once proclaimed that "I love Julia Roberts." I wasn't really serious. I was just caught up in the latest incredible performance of the talented Julia. As I thought about it, I came to the realization, "no I don't! I don't love Julia Roberts." The fact is I don't even know Julia Roberts. Except for what is shared in the tabloids or celebrity type magazines, which I rarely read, I don't know anything about her as a real person.

The truth is that I love "Pretty Woman," the role she played in that first film with Richard Geer in 1990. I loved Vivian Ward, the character Julia played, and the innocence and vulnerability she portrayed so well. This was another Cinderella story where every guy in the country, including me, just wanted to be her knight in shining armor, even riding to her rescue in a beautiful white stretch limousine.

I also love Erin Brockovich, her character in the film of the same name where Julia Roberts won an Oscar in 2001 for her leading role. Again, she was the beautiful, although rough-around-the-edges, white-trash single mom trying to make a difference against impossible odds as an assistant in a small-town law firm. I just admired the character so much and the strength and determination that made her successful, I couldn't help but love her too. She was gorgeous as usual. Come to think of it, I can't recall a movie where Julia Roberts didn't cause in me a heavy sigh and realization that she was a magnificent actor playing a new role, and that was the only way I would ever see her.

I loved Darby Shaw, the lead character in the 1993 movie "The Pelican Brief", playing opposite one of my all-time favorite male lead characters, Denzel Washington. Again, she was another beautiful, strong and brilliant "damsel in distress" trying to survive against the political and corporate corruption that tried to silence her. She just draws you in and makes you want to be the one to help save and protect her. Maybe I am a hopeless romantic, but I am so easily caught up in the story of her characters and her struggles to make a point. Ohh boy…..another heavy sigh for this guy. Be still, my heart.

I fell in love again with Anna Scott as the well-known celebrity trying to have a simple, anonymous relationship in Notting Hill. I believed, and still do, that a person of her celebrity status and world-renowned notoriety, would long for a more simple and anonymous existence away from the paparazzi and constant harassment by the media and general public. That is certainly understandable, if not for a long time, at least on an occasion where she could disappear into the landscape and be a normal person, free of the constant scrutiny and spotlight. Again, me and every other straight guy wanted to be the schmuck that came to her rescue.

As Julianne Potter in "My Best Friend's Wedding", she was the perfect girl-next-door friend that her best friend should have seen as "the one." What is the matter with these guys who don't see what is so obvious, but just bumble their way through life looking at the greener pastures in other women. Are they crazy? Don't they see this is Julia Roberts? It is perfectly clear to me from my comfortable arm chair. And, no matter how many times I watch the movie, the guy never figures it out. What a dummy.

I can't cover all the Julia Roberts movies I've seen, but I just wanted to make one more short comment about how much I enjoy watching her perform. I even loved her as Tinkerbell in the movie "Hook." She brings a magic to all her performances, and there is usually no ferry dust involved, just solid character acting at its finest. She is just so believable and fun to watch in any role, and her choice of movies guarantees success. Her beauty is timeless and she has such magical skills of engaging the audience, and in particular, me. By the way, have I told you I'm an incurable Julia Roberts fan? Hmmm. I don't know how you missed it.

I could spend a lot of time reviewing all the Julia Roberts movies I have seen over the years, but I can't do it and keep this chapter down to just a few pages. Ms. Roberts is such a skilled performer that I would be caught up in just about any role she took on. I think that what it comes down to is that I am in love with the brilliance of Julia Roberts' acting performances, for her characters and how she draws me into each and every story. I just want to defend or rescue her, sweeping her off her feet and carrying her away into a perfect fantasy life. Not going to happen. Again, heavy sigh. I'll be okay. I'll be okay.

No, I'm really not in love with Julia Roberts. However, I love her incredible acting skills and her effectiveness in bringing characters to life on the screen. Thank you Julia for all the emotions you've brought out of me through your gift of performance. I love you for that.

Turn In That Ticket
And be a winner

"If your ship doesn't come in, swim out to it."
Jonathan Winters

I'm reminded of a story I'd heard awhile back about a man who woke up every morning for weeks and the first thing he did was grab the morning newspaper to see if he'd won the most recent lottery. But so far, he hadn't. At first it was a casual activity, but over time it grew to be an obsession. As a matter of fact, as time went on, the obsession became a very intense ritual, so intense, he resorted to prayer. He believed that with God's help, certainly he would win. He even tried negotiating with God by suggesting that he would be satisfied with just a few million dollars and didn't necessarily need to win the great big two hundred million dollar lottery. After all, he wasn't a greedy man. However, he was in need and so he continued his daily ritual.

In the beginning, he would say a simple prayer at night before going to bed. As time went on and he didn't win, his prayer time would grow, both in duration and intensity. He moved from sitting on the edge of his bed to kneeling by his bed with his hands folded in reverence. Then his prayers grew to include singing, then chanting and beseeching God's help in total earnest. He even moved into the darkness and silence of his closet, where he kneeled down, looked up toward the heavens and coupled with pleadings and tears, made his most determined, emotional and desperate pleas.

This went on for weeks and months until finally one late night, he thought he heard God. As the man lay on the floor of his dark closet,

65

physically and emotionally exhausted, the closet started to shake like a small earthquake. A low rumbling noise began to fill the space and he could finally feel the presence of God. In an instant, all became quiet, just for a moment, as he heard the voice of God speaking clearly and distinctly to him. In a deep, resounding voice, God said, "Give me a break! Buy a ticket." I don't know if this man ever did win the lottery, but I think his chances were greatly improved by purchasing a ticket.

I have to admit, over the years, I have bought an occasional lottery ticket with the hopes of solving all of my financial problems in one such move. After all, somebody was going to win, and why not me? I was at least smart enough to buy a ticket and be in the game. As time went on, my optimism grew, as the jackpot amounts grew. When no one won the jackpot, it continued to grow even larger, sometimes into the three hundred, four hundred and five hundred million-dollar super lotteries.

I only bought tickets occasionally, sometimes one ticket, but usually two. I guess that was to double my odds, while only gambling with a small investment. After all, you only need one ticket to win.

Somewhere in this process, my goals changed. Initially, it was always about financial gain and being able to provide for me and my family. It would also help with college funds for my children, family trips, new homes and cars, and a lifestyle free of day to day stress of not having the choices that come with financial freedom.

I must have believed I could change my fortune and increase my odds by focusing on bigger and more lofty goals. I changed my mantra to something more along the lines of "just think about all the things I could fix in the community and the world, if I could just win the "big one." I'm smiling now because I feel a little bit silly that I think my good and noble intentions would make it happen. I guess I don't really believe it will make a difference in what I may win, if anything. But, it is an entertaining mental game to think about what I would do. Maybe someday I will know for sure. It could happen, couldn't it?

There is one realization I came to somewhere along the way. I would buy my two tickets, then place them in my wallet for safekeeping, with the hope of winning. And, I would hold onto the tickets for days or even weeks without checking to see if they were good, and if I had won something.

I didn't even want to look at the published numbers for fear that I might not win.

In thinking about it, I finally realized why I didn't want to know right away. This crazy thinking, or fearful mindset, is something we too often do in our lives that keeps us from moving forward. We're too afraid. My rationale was that if I didn't check the tickets today against the published numbers, I wouldn't know that I had already lost, which means I still had a chance to win. Not knowing gave me hope, albeit a false hope. If I didn't know, then there was still a chance, and I like to be pleasantly surprised.

In being totally honest with myself, I finally realized how crazy it is to think this way. It makes no sense. It means that I didn't really believe I was going to win after all. My hopes were crushed, my dreams were just dreams, and I was never going to really make a difference in the world. It also meant I was never going to be able to fix all the things I could fix if I had a couple hundred million dollars to work with. Winning the lottery would be an instant fix, which is what I was really hoping for. However, rarely does life work that way for anyone.

I have read many books and stories about very famous and successful people and how they started with nothing or very little but had a dream and worked hard to achieve that dream. They wanted to do something that would make their life better, provide for their family or other loved ones. But, the difference between them and most of us is they were willing to put in the work to reach the next milestone and continue toward their goals. They weren't looking for the quick fix, the instant fame and fortune, or the easy path to success. They were willing to work hard, do the research, develop their plans and implement a program or process that would lead them closer to their goals. They ran into a variety of obstacles and even potentially devastating circumstances, but they saw them as just hurdles to overcome. They understood those famous words from the movie, G.I. Jane, "What doesn't kill you makes you stronger." They stayed focused, adapted, did the work, overcame, changed directions or whatever it took, and pushed through to eventually succeed. With each challenge, they grew stronger.

I no longer count on or expect the Lottery to help achieve my goals in life. Instead, I am seriously and consistently engaging the disciplines of following my plan and putting in the work to help me achieve those things that are most important to me. My success doesn't have to be instant. I am more focused on enjoying the journey and the small successes along the way and what is most important to me. I've learned that it is not the reaching of the goal that provides the greatest satisfaction, although there is that. Rather, it is the journey, the path with all its forks, curves, obstacles, hills, valleys and rivers, including crooked sidewalks, that fuels the drive and re-enforces the sense of accomplishment.

Yes. On occasion, I still purchase two lottery tickets to ensure I have a shot, although it is a very long and possibly impossible shot, to win the BIG lottery. It takes so little effort, and as a form of justification, I'm supporting various education programs through the lottery.

Is it hypocritical? Probably! I still play the game. But when I do, I check the winning numbers immediately to see if I have won. If I haven't, I let go and get back to work. I intend to reach my goals whether I do it instantly through the lottery or through years of long and hard work. I am going to accomplish something and feel good about it along the way.

If you too play the lottery, be sure to turn in that ticket. You'll know then if you've won, or more likely, didn't. But, you will have your answer at that moment and can let go of the weight of "hoping" to win, and you can get to the work of moving toward and building your dream. With the same discipline every day, make that phone call, have that meeting, improve on your plan, share with your confidants, take the next step and keep falling or, failing forward. No matter how many times you fall, get up one more time. You may be surprised how close you are to winning.

Thrift Store Treasures

"Always do the right thing – that will gratify some of the people and astonish the rest."

Mark Twain

In life, sometimes, we are fortunate to go to work somewhere that is both noble and a fun place to be. In addition, we get to work for a boss that is demanding, but also fun and compassionate, and someone who lets you do your job to support the mission he leads.

I was especially fortunate because my boss gave me the freedom and the latitude to try new things and grow. During that experience, the boss was a Major Ed Henderson, administrator of The Salvation Army's Adult Rehabilitation Center in Orange County California. This program provides shelter, support, counselling and rehabilitation to many who are afflicted with the challenges of alcoholism and drug addiction. The Army's program works on the principle of the three-legged stool, the legs representing the body, the mind and the spirit. Take away any one of those legs and the stool does not work. It always fails and the stool falls down. The same thing could be said of a person.

The Salvation Army has many such programs throughout the world with an admirable level of success. In short, which is the relevant point of this story, as part of the rehabilitation and rebuilding process, all those in the program are assigned work responsibilities, generally in areas of their experience and background. Their work helps to process and restore usable discards that are donated by the community, which are then placed in thrift stores and sold to the public. This too, generates financial support for the whole program.

In my capacities, I had the opportunity to work with many of the men in the various departments and work centers, and seeing their skills and their recovery process was a blessing and an inspiration. These interactions provided for a number of interesting stories and treasures as I was to discover while going about my daily responsibilities.

There was a period of time when I was asked to supervise the warehouse operations while the general manager had to have surgery, which would keep him off work for almost three months. I was happy to shift my responsibilities because the operation was important and, it would give me an opportunity to experience our program from another perspective.

As the temporary Warehouse Manager, I'd spend time during the day walking through the work areas, including the sorting rooms, loading rooms and truck operations. One day as I was making my rounds, I observed one of our men throwing garbage and non-usable discards into the trash compactor, which was quite normal. Out of curiosity, I stopped and looked into the bottom of the bin, which was almost empty, and I saw a large, legal size, manila envelope lying at the bottom. It seemed odd to me that someone would throw anything away or donate something that might be of a legal document nature.

I reached into the bin and picked up the envelope and pulled out the contents. Much to my delight, I found that the enclosed papers were a hand-written score of the theme for the movie, Von Ryan's Express, which came out in 1965. The main stars of the movie were Frank Sinatra and Trevor Howard. The composer was Jerry Goldsmith, confirmed by his hand-written name on the score.

Being a musician, with a level of achievement with the guitar, trombone and baritone instruments, I had no problem reading the notes on the music and humming out the theme. I was in awe that the timing on the discovery of this envelope was just a minute or so before this work of art went into the trash compactor, on its way to a landfill somewhere, forever to be lost. Amazing! I think this has to be one of my most satisfying finds. This special piece of history was placed in the "collectible" section of our Antique Thrift Store where it would be more valued and sought after.

Another one of my responsibilities came about as a result of my background in areas of music, stage, video and film productions. The Major directed that any donations received relating to these areas, and ending up in the electronics shop, was to be brought to my attention. This was so I could evaluate the items and recommend a value for which it would be sold in the thrift stores. Working in this area was one of the highlights of my job and provided some memorable experiences.

For example, one day I was called to the electronics shop to look at a recent donation the shop worker had some questions about. When I arrived in the shop, I was pointed to a stack of fourteen large, sky blue, plastic cases, approximately fifteen by fifteen inches square in size. As I started looking at them to determine what they were, I first noticed the identification on the outside labels indicated they belonged to Disney Studios.

I opened one to find out that each case contained a two inch, thirty-six track, audio tape. As I learned more, I realized those fourteen containers were the master audio tapes for seven of Disneyland's two-hour music programs. This had to be one of the most questionable donations I think I had seen to date. In my mind, there was no way Disney Studios would dump these off in the form of a donation to anyone, including a reputable non-profit thrift store operation. Something wasn't right. This could not be a legitimate donation and I was determined to find out for sure.

That afternoon, I called Disney Studios and shared my story. They said they would get back to me. A week later, I hadn't heard from them, so I called them again. I shared my story again, and I was asked to wait while they transferred me to the legal department.

When someone new came on the line, I introduced myself again and started to relate my story. I was quickly cut off, and the person on the other end of the line said: "Boy, do you know how to stir things up, up here!" I asked what he meant by that, and he related to me they had been looking for those tapes for quite some time. Oh, yes, and they were very pleased I had called. So was I.

The story that was related to me was that the tapes were indeed master audio tapes for seven musical productions at Disneyland, in Anaheim, California. They had been kept at a company that specialized in storing audio, film and video masters. But, when the company went out of business, no one could account for the tapes and they somehow ended up in the form of a donation to our center. Disney Studios was very grateful, and immediately sent a couple of producers down to collect the tapes from my office. Because we were a non-profit organization, they also brought a donation check to say "thank you" for seeing the value and rescuing the tapes and getting them back to Disney. I was right about my concern for the legitimacy of the donation, and we were pleased to return them to their rightful owners. Besides, we are all Disney fans, right?

Later that year, I stumbled on another unusual donation, at least in my mind. As I passed through the Electronics Shop, I noticed a few sixteen-millimeter reels of film stacked on the incoming rack of donations. Since I had done a lot of audio/visual activities in school, it made me pause to see what they were. Only one of the reels was in a canister, but I could see it was a film titled The Real McCoys. What? This popular series ran from nineteen fifty-seven through nineteen sixty-three, starring Walter Brennan, Richard Crenna and Kathleen Nolan. I loved that program when I was a kid.

I took the reels back to my office for further examination using a film projector I had there. Some reels were not marked, so I had to roll them out and look at the leader part of the film and found the name of the film. Two of the reels also included the word "Pilot."

As you may know, the "Pilot" of a film is the first episode shown to help determine if there is interest in developing a series. In short, I ended up with three reels of the show "The Real McCoys", one being "the pilot", another being the first episode and the third being "the pilot" dubbed in Spanish. This wasn't the end. In fact, it was the beginning of a new adventure.

Over the year, many gracious and generous celebrities have given their support and assistance to The Salvation Army, and it gave me an idea. If I could get in touch with Richard Crenna, who played the character Luke in the show, I might be able to make another friend for our organization. Many celebrities have collections of their careers, and I felt these reels were unique to the history of the series, and maybe Mr. Crenna would have some interest in acquiring them. When I contacted his office, his assistant told me he wasn't in, but that he would call me as soon as possible.

Mr. Crenna did call my home one evening, but I was not yet home. My oldest daughter answered the phone and when Mr. Crenna asked to speak to me, she informed him that I wasn't home, so he asked her to relay the message. My daughter was only nine years old, and when my wife asked her who had called, Kristie told her it was Richard Crenna. Kristie wouldn't know who Richard Crenna was, but my wife sure did. It was quite a surprise to Jan, who then wished she had answered the phone. She had met him some years earlier when she was in her late teens, and she was a fan.

The next day I finally connected with Mr. Crenna himself and I told him what I had found. He told me about his personal collection of meaningful career memorabilia and was grateful that I had thought of him. Arrangements were made and the films were sent off to him. It seemed like a good place for them to go, and again, we were happy to share them with him.

One of my favorite personal finds happened on a day off when my wife and I were out and about and decided to stop into a local thrift store as a lazy afternoon diversion. While looking around, exploring what treasures might be found, I spied a framed picture of a small sail boat resting lazily on the edge of the shore. Having served in the Navy and the Coast Guard, most things nautical get my attention.

When I walked up to the picture, I noticed the glass was dirty and the bottom corner was also cracked. Still, the picture intrigued me and the frame and matting were in good shape. I asked the clerk if they had some glass cleaner and a rag so I could clean it before making a decision. They were originally asking five dollars for the framed painting, but today it had been marked down to three dollars and fifty cents. While I was waiting for the cleaner, I had a few moments to thoroughly examine the art, and I noticed a few additional things.

First, it appeared to be a lithograph of an original painting, and was hand numbered as a number two hundred and sixty-eight out of two hundred and seventy-five. It was also signed at the bottom by the artist, *E Vial Hugas*. The name didn't mean anything to me or ring any bells, not that it should. However, I was pleasantly surprised when I turned the painting over and found a couple of things glued to the back that gave me some answers and piqued my interest even more.

The artist's name was Eduardo Vial Hugas and I learned he is a relatively famous painter from Spain. There was an attached article describing his life and many of the awards and recognitions he had received as an artist. In addition, glued to the back of the picture, was a certificate of Authentication from the *Societe de Verification de la Nouvelle Gravure Internationale of New York and Paris,* in association with the Collector's Guild of New York, NY. I don't know what all that means, but it sounded important, so, I bought the painting and took it home.

I've since replaced the glass. Later, I asked a friend of mine who is associated with the local art institute in Portland, Oregon, to show the lithograph to a curator he knows. When he got back to me, he told me the lithograph was valued at about eight hundred dollars. Wow! That was a nice discovery. The beautiful lithograph had caught my eye and I still have it hanging in my home office today, along with many of my other nautical and collectible pieces. There are other such stories that could be shared at another time.

Not every find in a thrift store is a treasure or a valuable piece of art as I was fortunate to find so many years ago. Some were just good and practical items I needed, but at a greatly discounted price. However, it may be a valuable treasure to you in some way. You just never know what you are going to find when searching through thrift store or garage sale merchandise. The other thing to keep in mind is that these items change weekly, and you never know what new treasure will arrive in their next store delivery. That is part of the fun of just going back occasionally and seeing what there is to see. Who knows? You may just stumble across or find that special treasure you have always been looking for. It could happen.

While I was working at The Salvation Army Thrift Shop operation, an acquaintance once asked me why I didn't hang on to some of these great finds myself, and maybe one day sell them to a collector. As I shared with him, "They weren't mine." I know that sounds simple, but it really is that simple. I was raised that what was mine was mine, and what wasn't mine wasn't mine. It belonged to someone else, so just because I held them in my hands and could see the value, it still didn't mean I could take them and make them mine. A quote I adopted many, many years ago is: "Integrity is doing the right thing when you know no one else is watching." My parents taught me that principle. Besides, I could fool a lot of people a lot of the time, but I can never deceive God, so what is the point. Doing the right thing is always the right thing.

One final thought. As a result of these four examples of Thrift Store

Treasures, though there are many more, there is one remaining question that has haunted my mind to this day. I'll say it in short, then I'll say it again. What have we missed? What wonderful, beautiful, valuable, historic treasure has slipped through the fingers of our discerning eyes and sorting process, and is now gone forever? I don't know, and I guess I really don't want to know. It could keep me up at night for the rest of my life, and life is too short. We do the best we can, when we have the opportunity. So, check it out. Take the family on an adventure, or treasure hunt, and visit your local thrift stores. You may find that one man's trash is another man's treasure. It certainly is a life-long lesson and it is interesting to think about why some people value what someone else may not. It's actually fun to find out. Good luck and good treasure hunting.

It's Just A Penny

"No one can make you feel inferior without your permission."

Eleanor Roosevelt

I think it was Benjamin Franklin who said, "A penny saved is a penny earned." I suppose that is true, after all, Mr. Franklin was a smart man.

In another way, I like to think that a penny found is a raise. It is also a gift, which I'll explain a bit later and I believe it will make sense at that time. But first, let me give you some background of the value of picking up a penny.

When I was a kid, starting in elementary school and going through high school, it was not cool to bend over and pick up a penny. I never understood that attitude, but you know how peer pressure can affect the thinking of a child during their growing up years.

There was a time when if you spotted a penny on the ground and you bent over to pick it up, someone on the playground might laugh at you for doing that and even begin to ridicule you for it. I can only imagine that it was because they felt you must be so poor or inadequate to find it necessary to bend over and pick something up off the ground. To do so supposedly labeled you as a lower class, white trash, poor person from a lesser family, not worthy of respect or valued for your thriftiness.

For a long while, I think that when I saw a penny on the ground, I looked around to see if anyone was watching before I picked it up. I may have even bent down to tie my shoe so no one would know that it was really to pick up that copper coin. After all, it was just a penny.

Some years later, as I grew and matured, I realized how dumb that was, and how embarrassed I felt that I was so easily manipulated into thinking that picking up a penny or any other coin was some kind of demeaning act. At that point, I was determined to not care what anyone else thought and to make the effort to pick up anything of value regardless of its monetary significance.

It may have been a level of rebellion, but I learned later that this act was more important and rewarding than I thought it could ever be. I'll even admit there were times when things were so tight financially I found it necessary and helpful to pick up any coin on the ground that came within my awareness. What changed my whole outlook on this subject came in the form of a story about a very rich man who also picked up pennies he found along the way.

As I recall the story, there was a well-respected and very wealthy businessman who was leaving his office one day with a few of his younger executives walking with him. After just a few steps outside of his enormous office building, he stopped walking and paused for just a moment before crouching down to pick up a very shiny penny that was on the sidewalk in front of him.

He picked it up, stood up and seemed to be contemplating the find before moving on. One of his executives asked him why he bothered to stop and pick up the penny when he was such a successful and wealthy man. As he turned to address the young executive, he reached in his pocket and pulled out the penny. In showing it to him, he asked him what he saw. As expected, the young executive, a bit embarrassed, started describing the penny. It is mostly copper, like most of the billions of pennies in circulation, shinier than most and worth just one hundredth of a dollar. He didn't add what he was also thinking, and that is that it is worth so little that it wasn't worth his time or effort to take the moment and bend over to pick it up.

With a patient voice, the wealthy man said, "You missed the most important point." He then turned the coin face up and pointed just above the head of President Abraham Lincoln, to the words on the coin. It says, "In God We Trust." For the wealthy gentleman, the most important point of the process was the written reminder he received each time he picked up a penny. It wasn't the amount or value of the coin, but the value of the message stamped onto the coin.

Before hearing that story, true or not, I picked up a penny, a nickel, a dime or any other amount of currency because it made sense to me. It had value, regardless of the amount. That story has stuck with me for all these years, but now I pick up pennies because of the message "In God we trust." It is a constant reminder of my life and the strength that is given to me every day to keep going, working, trying, giving, receiving and so much more. It is my trust in God that makes all things possible. If God be for me, who can be against me? My answer is "nobody."

It is interesting how many pennies I have picked up over the years. I have no idea, but I am confident it is into the thousands. Again, it's not the monetary value but the message and inspiration I receive from it. I don't go around looking on the ground for pennies, but they always seem to be shiny and stand out. I have to laugh sometimes when I find them because of the most illogical places where they would show up.

Sometimes, I'll stop at a rest stop or gas station during my travels, and as I am getting out of the car, there is a penny on the ground. One time as I was getting out of the car, I noticed a penny on the asphalt. Then I noticed another one near it. Then I noticed another and then another and then more, for a total of eighteen pennies, all within a six-foot radius just outside the door of my car. Anymore, it seems that I find one just about every day. Not always, but pretty frequently. It is a fun pastime and surprise, never knowing when they are going to show up, but I look forward to the special message reminder each time they do.

Now, when I see a penny on the ground, even before I pick it up, I get a smile on my face and I am grateful for this country that allows me the religious freedom to believe in the God I know and trust. It warms my heart every time and I treat that penny as today's gift in the form of a reminder. I don't mind stopping to pick it up, reading the words and putting the joyful coin in my pocket. In fact, I enjoy it and look forward to it. It also settles my day and helps me focus on what is most important in life, and I believe it lifts my spirit in so many ways. So, it is not just a penny, but it is so much more.

Not All Green Lights

"There are no shortcuts to any place worth going."
Beverly Sills

I grew up as a teenager in southern California, so when I was old enough to start driving and finally got my license, I learned to drive all over, eventually mastering the Los Angeles freeway systems. As complicated as they were back then, they didn't even compare to the number of freeway configurations that now cross the metropolitan Los Angeles basin, a real challenge to the "newbies" that find themselves caught up in the LA traffic patterns of today. It was horrific then, and even worse today.

At one point in my life, I moved from southern California to Dallas, Texas to take a job there, which got me out of the LA traffic routine and I could feel a sense of relief. The traffic in the Dallas and Fort Worth area was so much lighter than it was in southern California. However, one of the main complaints I heard about living in Dallas from the locals is how bad the traffic is. I just had to laugh because I thought to myself, "They really have no idea."

A few years later, I took a new position with the company, but had to re-locate to Portland, Oregon. The traffic in Portland was so much better than it had been in Dallas. Once again, however, one of the main complaints that I heard most from the people in the Portland area was how awful the traffic was. Again, I just had to laugh because they also had no idea what the traffic was like in Dallas, let alone how it was in the Los Angeles area. I guess, like most of life is, things are relative and traffic congestion is in the eye of the beholder, or the driver, and attitude is everything.

Being on the freeways is one thing, but being on city streets can be quite another, also extremely congested and often times frustrating. Have you ever noticed how traffic lights can really impact your life for the good, or they can be a real irritation? I am pretty confident in saying that we have all experienced it to varying degrees.

Even though street lights are designed to assist the flow of traffic in all directions, they sometimes don't appear to be anything but an obstacle that impedes your movement toward your desired destination. This has really created a hot button and trigger point for some people who find themselves at the mercy of the traffic signal system.

Over the years, I have observed a whole array of behaviors. Even before I was driving, I observed how the tedium of driving from point A to point B and then to point C, could cause some people to become a different person altogether when behind the steering wheel of a car. Some even appear to transform or mutate into an unrecognizable species when life is happening and traffic isn't flowing to their advantage. I must admit, at times, that was me until I acknowledged I didn't want to be like that and I could not let things I can't control, control me.

However, that doesn't mean I didn't try or have my moments. I would even later have to acknowledge that I didn't handle it as well as I could have. Still, some drivers even took the opportunity to acknowledge my patience and driving expertise by using that international single finger hand signal to tell me, "you're number one", or at least that is how I chose to interpret the gesture.

I tried a variety of strategies to assist my travel and the flow of traffic. One of those attempts was through sheer will power. I would concentrate and command a red light to turn green, or if the light was green, I would will it to stay green or wait for me. These attempts rarely worked or changed the light pattern. However, on occasion the light would change in my favor following one of my commands and I would quietly take credit for having willed it. Pure coincidence, I'm sure. That reminds me that even a broken clock is right twice a day.

When things weren't working out, I would try something as simple as twitching my nose like Samantha did in the TV show *Bewitched*. It always worked for her, but for me, sometimes it would work, but most of the time, it was just a funny exercise.

I even found myself talking directly to the lights, the inanimate objects along my path, seeking sympathy and understanding. However, I never resorted to begging or tears. That seemed a bit over the line. I was also very polite and would use words like please and thank you. If I needed a green light, the response "please" was appropriate to the asking. When the light changed in my favor, a "thank you" was automatic. Maybe I believe good karma was a useful expectation. Who knows, but it was worth a try.

I also began to learn which lights were "smart lights" in my community, which gave me the opportunity to anticipate or plan my flow around town. With sensors set in the road, along with the appropriate programming, the lights would respond to the road activity and change to accommodate the flow of traffic activity at those intersections.

Over the years, I may have put way too much thought into traffic flow and how the lights would affect that flow, but as my older brother would say, "that is the scientist in me."

Having tried almost everything I could come up with, I finally found a formula that works for me and has made all the difference in the world. I am much more patient, understanding and relaxed, and have a lot less stress in my life. My travels, even short ones across town, are more enjoyable and less aggravating. I arrive at my destinations on time, relaxed, pleasant, and much happier than I used to. The crazies on the road no longer determine my day or my life, and I believe I am healthier and enjoy my life more because of this new approach.

It is so simple and I am surprised it took me so long to figure it out. The simple act of acknowledging that life happens and life is not all green lights. Sometimes, the lights are red and stop or delay us along the road. Sometimes the lights are yellow, giving us warnings or cautions that affect what we do. On rare occasions, all lights are green and things go just the way we want them to.

The trip is quick, enjoyable and without incident. At these times, if we even notice, we can enjoy the perfection of the moment. I've learned to accept each trip as just that, a journey to some destination and things happen along the way. As I've heard so many times before, it is the journey, not the destination. I settle my mind to accept the environment and obstacles along the way regardless of whether my trip is affected by lights, accidents, rush hour traffic, construction or even weather as I travel along the way. Arriving safely at my destination is paramount, always. It also helps to plan your trip and allow yourself the time to reach your destination on time, or even early.

In short, it all comes down to being in control of those things within your power to control, and not to stress over those things you cannot control. If there is a secret to success, it can be summed up in one word, and that word is "attitude." The right attitude and being in the right mindset can make all the difference in the world. With the right attitude, even not having all green lights will no longer matter. You will enjoy whatever you are doing so much more, and life as a whole, will be so much better.

Down From the Mountain Top
The Glen Eyrie Experience

"The purpose of life is to matter – to count, to stand for something, to have it make a difference that we lived at all."
Leo Rosen

I'd been looking forward to it for the past three years. I had heard it from so many friends about how much they enjoyed their experience at Glen Eyrie and how their lives had been changed, never again to be the same. I couldn't wait.

Ever since Jan and I found out a couple of months earlier that we had been selected and would be going, I felt like a little kid waiting to take his first trip to camp. I was ready! My heart was excited, and at the same time, longing for everything the experience would have to offer, and the Lord knew I was ready and willing. He also knew exactly what I needed, and that I needed to share this time with Jan.

As members of The Salvation Army church, each year, selected young and mature couples are invited to attend a week of evangelistic training and spiritual renewal at a retreat center in Colorado Springs, Colorado.

The "it" I'd been so anxiously waiting for was Glen Eyrie. Well, actually, that was the name of the location just outside the city of Colorado Springs, Colorado. The "it" was the Soldiers National Seminar on Evangelism (S.N.S.E.). Come to think of it, everyone I've ever heard talk about it refers to the "it" as Glen Eyrie. The Officer of the Day welcomed us all to S.N.S.E., pronounced "sneezy."

What you have to realize is that I had been looking forward to this special week as a very much needed spiritual retreat. Upon arriving in the beautiful hills of Colorado Springs and entering the gates of the site known as "Glen Eyrie," my heart rejoiced. I had this wonderful feeling that God was there, and that He had been awaiting my arrival. I was very excited and more specifically, completely open to the wonderful experiences that lay ahead. I wanted to take in everything that was available. At this point, I wasn't completely clear on the evangelistic emphasis of the conference, for I was really focused on the spiritual retreat that I so desperately needed.

It was apparent right away that this was going to be a wonderful week as each of us were so warmly greeted by the staff Welcome Committee. We checked in, picked up our room keys and seminar kits, and headed for our very comfortable accommodations. As Jan and I walked into our room, as nice a hotel room as I've stayed in, I was surprised to find there was no television, no radio, and no telephone. But, then again, perhaps I wasn't surprised. I'm not as slow as it might first seem, as I very quickly ascertained there was a purpose for the non-availability of these commonplace distractions. This was a number of years before cell phones. Not having such communication devices to keep contact with the outside world allowed us to completely focus on God and the topics of the conference. What an unexpected blessing.

I could spend the next several pages telling you about our busy schedule of required and elective classes, like Person to Person Evangelism, Young Adult Evangelism, Penitent Form Counseling, Child Evangelism and many others. They were all excellent sessions, and with the quality of instructors that Jan and I experienced, it was very apparent that God had His hand on the choosing of the staff.

I'm sure the message presented by each instructor and general session speakers was received by each delegate in a clearly personal way. As for myself, it was as though they were speaking directly to me. Each one had prepared specifically the message for me that the Lord had brought me to Glen Eyrie to hear. Perhaps this was the only way He could get me to sit down long enough for me to listen. And listen I did, at every opportunity.

All too soon it seemed, the reality of Saturday morning was upon us. Who could have believed that seven days had passed so quickly since our arrival? With covenants signed the night before, and farewell hugs being shared among newly made friends, it was time to head down from the mountain. It took several heavy sighs and a few tears to say good-by and start the trip home.

At this point, I think the fears and anticipation were even greater than they were before assaulting the city of Colorado Springs with open air services and door to door evangelism. Oh yes, we were excited about the wonderful experience we had enjoyed on the mountain top, the overwhelming closeness to God we had felt, and the new confidence we had gained for sharing the gospel. But now it was time to go back down the mountain to our individual churches, back to the work place, and back to our family and friends.

We were nervous. We knew that unless they had experienced such a week as this, even our loved ones wouldn't understand how we felt and how our lives had been changed. They may not understand the spiritual growth that had taken place in just one week's time. In all probability, when we would try to tell them, their response would be something like, "Oh, that's nice," and give us that caring, blank look.

I guess that really isn't the important issue here. What is important is there was a change, a marvelous renewing of the spirit, and a newly dedicated focus and direction in our Christian lives. Jan and I know there was a wonderful change, and God knows. My prayer is that those who know us will also sense that change has occurred and, the Holy Spirit would prompt them to ask us about it.

Nervous? Yes. Anticipating? Yes. But, I know that I go in the strength of the Lord, with the assurance that I will never be alone. Jesus made a promise in the book of Matthew when he said, "Lo, I am with you always, even unto the end of the age." That's good enough for me. I learned a new chorus while on the mountain top, and it really summarized the change in my heart. It goes like this:

Here am I Lord, It Is I Lord, I have heard you calling in the night.
I will go Lord, if you lead me, I will hold your people in my heart.

Praise God. I had a wonderful, life changing experience at the S.N.S.E. He blessed me like I never thought possible. I know that I can't stay on the mountain top, for God's workers are needed down in the fields, in the valleys and in the cities. But, I'll never forget Glen Eyrie and the conference staff that poured out their hearts to share God's wonderful love with me. They sure did. And just like my friends had told me, my life was changed, never again to be the same.

Crossing the Line

Webster's New World College Dictionary defines "tradition" as: "the handing down orally of stories, beliefs, customs, etc. from generation to generation" or, "a historical line of conventions, principles, or attitudes characteristics of a school, social group, movement, etc." or, "the long-established custom or practice having the precedent or unwritten law." In my mind, the organizations that exemplify this definition to the greatest degree are represented by our military branches of service.

Each branch is steeped in traditions that have been carried down through the years and is an integral part of their very existence, greatly contributing to the standards, myths and legends that strengthen the whole in so many ways. One such tradition for the maritime services, and in my case the Navy, is the "Crossing the Line" ceremony.

I was aboard the USS Richard B Anderson, the Navy Destroyer I was assigned to, and we were in transit to the City of Penang, Malaysia and then on to Singapore. We had spent quite a period of time at sea already and this was going to be a chance to visit a foreign port and to, in essence, show the flag. We were all looking forward to a few days of rest and sightseeing, as well as visiting and socializing with some of our Australian allies that were based there.

During our years homeported in Japan and spending most of our time off the east coast of Viet Nam, this was the first time we had traversed so far south and near the equator. So, our Captain decided he would vary our course to a little farther south in order for the crew to be able to have the knowledge and experience of crossing the equator, which was traditionally referred to as "Crossing the Line." In so doing, this direction change provided the opportunity for all of us, the un-initiated, to experience the long-standing tradition of "Crossing the Line." My understanding and recollection goes something like this.

In the tradition of the Navy, a seaman, officer or enlisted, who has never crossed the equator is considered a "Polliwog," which we all know as a tadpole. These creatures are the "newbies" of the aquatic world and are weak with no backbones and have not earned the privilege of becoming a "Shellback." The Shellback has the strength, durability and longevity of a full-grown sea turtle. Having that protective shell has to be earned, and in order to achieve that designation, an individual has to endure the rigors of the "Crossing the Line" ceremony and traditional hazing. On our ship, this was a two-day event.

Disclosure: Let me make it perfectly clear at this point in this Politically Correct world that participating in the ceremony is strictly voluntary. Everyone has the opportunity to participate, but no one is mandated or required to be involved. It is an individual's choice.

As we were approaching the equator, about a day out from the crossing, the initiation began. All sailors participated in the ceremony, including officers. I was a young ensign, having only been on board a little over a year, but there was no way I was NOT going to be included in whatever the hazing entailed. If I were smarter, I may have not chosen to make myself stand out in the way I did, but for me, it was more about wanting to push back a little in the face of the career Shellbacks that would be in charge of the ceremony.

What I did was to put on my khaki pants and a white t-shirt as my uniform of the day. But, what I added to push back was to take a black permanent marker and yellow highlighter pen to print ensign boards on the shoulders of my very white and clean t-shirt. In short, I was shoving it in their face, daring them to try and break me. As Popeye would say, "I ams what I am, and that's all what I am. YukYukYukYukkkkk!" At one point, a senior Shellback approached and informed me "that was a big mistake, Sir." So it began.

Regardless of the initiation, we were still required to perform our regular duties and stand our watches as scheduled. However, when we were off duty, we were fair game.

I had finished my evening watch on the bridge and headed to my stateroom and my bed, affectionately known as "the rack", to get some sleep before my bridge watch in the morning. I was comfortably settled and had fallen to sleep when at about zero dark thirty, two Shellbacks entered my room and ordered me to report to the forecastle (front) of the ship to stand my equator watch. As directed, I got up, put on my uniform of the day and headed topside. I was in my khaki pants, painted t-shirt and a pair of flip flops. Because I had the "equator" watch, I had to lie on the deck at the foremost front of the ship, face down with my head and shoulders through the bull nose of the ship. It was my responsibility to look down at the ocean and to alert the Captain when we crossed the equator. Yep. That is what I was to do, and that is exactly what I did.

It couldn't have been a more perfect night to stand this watch as we transited the ocean of the south Pacific. The sky was clear, the moon was full, and the sea was perfectly calm. It was so gorgeous, calming and memorable I could have stayed there all night, and probably would have fallen asleep. But, there was more to it as I was to find out.

While prone on the metal deck at the front of the ship, every five minutes, a couple of Shellbacks would turn on a fire hose and hose me down. So, as relaxed as I may have been, I was soaking wet, and cold, and wide awake. Just as I would start to warm up, they came back and hosed me down again. I guess they didn't get it right the first few times. Regardless, I continued to watch for the equator and to provide my reports. This went on for what seemed like quite a while, but I recall it was probably less than thirty minutes. After all, they had other Polliwogs that needed to do their time. Not so bad.

The next day, as I made my rounds, I observed other Polliwogs engaged in various forms of crossing the line duties, some more challenging than others, but still testing our metal. Around noon, the announcement was made that we had successfully crossed the equator and that all Polliwogs were to report the bow of the ship.

We didn't know what that meant until we arrived there and were ordered to get on our hands and knees. We were about to crawl the gauntlet with various physical trials along the way. The gauntlet stretched the length of the ship, all the way to the fantail (rear of the ship) where the final initiation ceremonies would be completed. The USS Anderson was three hundred and ninety feet in length. At this point, since I was on my hands and knees, with my head down, I can only recount my personal experience.

The crawl to the fantail was about three hundred feet for me, the length of a football field. The deck, however, is covered with a paint material called "non-skid" because it is laced with sand to make the surface rough and to make it easier to walk the deck without slipping in heavy seas. However, crawling on this surface can be a little more challenging for your hands and knees, knees especially. Periodically, along the journey, each Polliwog would receive a swat from the offended Shellbacks. The swats were tolerable, and I finally stopped counting. I just knew I was half way there.

There was a point about mid-ship when I received "extra special" treatment as part of my initiation. It will make more sense to you to know that my assignment aboard the Anderson was as the Main Propulsion Officer. My responsibilities were to oversee the engine rooms, the boiler rooms and all related spaces that provided for the propulsion of the ship. At that time, the Anderson ran on black oil. This oil was dark and thick and was burned in the boilers to create the steam that drove the ship. We referred to it as black oil, or Bunker C, because it was the darkest and crudest oil the Navy provided for our older ships.

As I reached about two thirds of the way to the fantail, I felt someone pulling up on the back of my pants and underwear, exposing my butt crack. My shirt was already untucked as I made my way aft. I looked around just as two of my boiler crew started pouring two gallons of this black oil down the back of my pants. Instantly, every crack and crevice of my nether regions were engulfed in this dark and stinky substance, drenching my pants and shorts as it drained down my thighs and legs while I continued my crawl toward final judgement. The "black oiling" I received, and it is my belief, I was the only person that experienced this special honor. It was also accompanied by two swats. To this day, I'm not sure if I was given this special treatment because they hated me or because they loved me. I want to believe they loved me and I was special. That is what I kept telling myself.

At this point, I was now almost to the back of the ship. I noticed that the knees of my pants were worn and torn by now. The non-skid really did its work. In addition, I was aware of the blood on my hands and knees as a result of the gauntlet crawl over the past forty-five minutes. The abrasions were painless and the bleeding was minor. I'd done worse as a kid falling off my bike. "I'm almost there."

When I arrived at the fantail, I continued my crawl through a few minor obstacles, the worst being the enclosed garbage chute we had to crawl through to get all the way on to the fantail. It was slippery and tolerable except for the smell of puke deposited there by a few of my shipmates who'd made the journey ahead of me. After completing a few additional stations to perform a series of sit-ups, push-ups and squats, a senior Shellback lifted me to my feet and led me to the final challenge. I could see what was coming and this may have been the worst.

I was directed to kneel in front of the biggest Shellback on the ship, seated on his throne, complete with a royal scepter (also known as a toilet plunger), wearing only a bedsheet for a diaper. They said he was Neptune's baby and before I completed my initiation, I had to "kiss the belly" of Neptune's baby. That would have been easy enough except that the huge, hairy, bare belly was covered in mustard and some other unidentifiable goo. At this point, it was time to be done. I crawled forward to kiss the baby's belly. As I dutifully complied, the baby grabbed the back of my head giving my face a good smothering and belly rub to complete my initiation. As I finally stood up and wiped away the mess on my face, I was congratulated and proclaimed as the newest Official Shellback in the Navy.

I was done. I completed the initiation with pride, endurance and resolve, and now I could relax and get cleaned up. As I started along the deck heading to my stateroom and shower, I realized my shirt was destroyed and my pants were no longer wearable. So, in the middle of the South Pacific Ocean, I stood on the deck, stripped my clothes and offered them to Davy Jones' Locker. The only thing that was covering me at this time was the black oil that had saturated my private areas and my no longer tidy whities. I was physically and emotionally drained as I stepped into a nice warm shower to try and remove the black oil still clinging to my skin. In reality, it took three showers to feel clean enough to put on some fresh clothes.

Am I glad I participated in this initiation? That is affirmative. It was a tradition I wanted to be a part of and a goal I wanted to achieve. It was an experience that I will never forget, and I can look back on with fondness and a smile. I did it, as did many others of the crew. Today, they'd call it a male bonding experience. So be it.

I later received a beautiful and official certificate commemorating the transition from a polliwog to a Shellback. Now, I am and will forever be a Shellback. Can you say that? Maybe someday you'll have the opportunity. If you do, go for it. You will never forget the experience.

In short, as a friend and mentor once said to me: "Sometimes, the most tortuous of life's offerings also provide the warmest and most rewarding memories. Never shy from the necessary to avoid the uncomfortable." That is good, sound advice.

One, Two Three...Too Late

*"The objective of teaching a child is to enable him to get
along without his teacher."*

Anonymous

Raising children is a gift, but also a grave responsibility and is not for the faint hearted. Although we benefit from having parents that show us so many things about raising us and our siblings, when it comes time to be on our own, it can be like learning on the job. We've learned that every child is unique and different from our other children and as there are a lot of basic similarities among the children, we still may have to adapt as we raise each successive child.

There are numerous books that help us understand the differences between the first child, the number two child, and the subsequent number three or more siblings. In addition, what about the difference between twins, including the variables that comes with identical twins or twins of differing sex? Wow. That is a lot to consider, so off we go on our journey of doing the best we can with the knowledge and limited experience that we currently have in our bag of tricks.

One of the child-rearing challenges for me was, with all the variables and environments, the question was how best to most effectively discipline your children? Which technique works best for the second child after your first attempts with the first child were successful, or maybe not? Once again, you have the basics, so you adapt and do the best you can under the circumstances while on the job. Hopefully, the parents who are raising and disciplining the children are adults already.

Based on my upbringing, the general technique that I believe works best is to set parameters of behavior and guide the children in that direction. This also means clear, understandable parameters so the child knows when they might exceed the parameters and what the consequences of exceeding them will mean. Of course, as the children grow and develop, the parameters will generally expand to give them greater latitude.

One key to making this work is CONSISTENCY in all stages of the process. The parameters must be clear and consistent and not vary on a whim. If there is a logical reason to vary them, it must be clear as to why the variation and, whether it is permanent or if they return to the basic parameters again at some point.

It is also important there is consistency in the punishment that is handed out in response when punishment is warranted, and commensurate with the severity of the violation. I know this all sounds rather official or unnecessarily regimented, but I like to keep in mind that these are helpful guidelines. It is important to be sure that the penalties are consistent and fair, and not excessive. It's a fine balance, even an art, to make the point without going overboard. Call it tough love, but necessary.

There was a time when my oldest child was testing the system. She was about eleven and feeling her independence when she decided to misbehave at dinner one evening. I don't recall the specifics of the offense, but I explained to her why she was out of line and the potential consequences of her actions if she didn't correct them. I also pointed out that was her first warning.

As dinner continued, she continued to misbehave and showed an unwillingness to comply with my instructions. Soon, thereafter, I gave her a second warning and she seemed to modify her behavior in a positive direction, at least for a short time. Then, she was back to misbehaving and pretty much disregarding my instructions with no change or effort to comply. At that point, I gave her a third and final warning and she still had a chance to recover and stop the coming discipline. Nothing changed, at which point, much to her horror, I got up from my chair and stepped toward her end of the table.

That was the point when she realized she had gone too far, and her pleading for grace began in earnest. "Daddy, daddy, daddy, I'm sorry. Daddy, daddy, I won't do it again." She was sincere as she continued to plead her case to not be disciplined, even to the point of genuine tears.

Unfortunately for her, it was too late. I pointed out that she had pushed it to the point of causing me to get out of my dinner chair, so she missed her chance, three times, to adjust her behavior.

The punishment consisted of two swats to her behind. There is plenty of padding there and the pain is temporary. I know to some, this sounds a bit harsh or maybe even abusive, but it wasn't. It was two swats with my hand and not a beating. Neither me nor my wife would ever beat our children, which they will attest to, but a swat or two was an appropriate response to the level of the offense. The discipline was swift and effective and there was never a need again for me to have to get out of my chair. The message was clear and both my daughters understood it because it is simple and straightforward. The offense was made. The warnings were given. The discipline followed commensurate with the offense, and the drama was over. The love remained and things were good and the incident was never brought up again. Well, not exactly.

Nine years after our second daughter was born, we were blessed with a baby boy. That was one of the most wonderful and meaningful events of my life. I was perfectly happy and content that my first two children were girls and perfect in every way I could imagine. However, when my wife gave me a boy, it opened a whole new world of appreciation, commitment and responsibility that took my life to a new level of fatherhood. I was grateful beyond belief and his birth gave me opportunities to grow in ways still yet unimagined. Life was very good.

When my son was about eight years of age, an event started to repeat itself one evening at dinner. If you've heard this story before, don't stop me. We were sitting around the dinner table when my son decided to test the system for getting away with bad behavior. Sound familiar. So, being consistent in my approach, I let him know that his behavior was unacceptable and that he needed to stop. That was his first warning.

Again, it worked for a few minutes then he was back at it, pushing the limits. I explained that the potential for going down the path he had chosen was not going to lead to a good end. He got his second warning, yet he continued. As I began to explain, for the third time the errors of his ways, I didn't have a chance to finish my speech. At the exact same moment, both of my daughters, shouted out in unison, "Don't make dad get up from his chair." It was hilarious as my wife and I both busted out in laughter and went on praising the girls for looking out for their younger brother. It worked. We never got through the third warning, and there was no reason to complete the process. The message was re-enforced by his protective older siblings. It's a funny story we still love sharing.

As a parent and a father, I may have not done everything right as I raised my children, but like most parents, I did the best I could with the training and experience I had and gained in the process of being a parent. Key for me was always being clear about the parameters of what was expected, and the consistency and fair discipline when those limits were exceeded. Discipline was always delivered with love, and grace and forgiveness always followed immediately. I am pleased with the loving, caring and compassionate adults my children have become and I am especially proud of their success in their own lives and families. Even as a grandparent, it has never again been necessary to resort to the "One, Two Three – Too Late" approach to discipline, and I am grateful for that.

Ain't No Big Ting Bruddah!

"The greatest mistake you can make in life is to be continually fearing you will make one."

H. Hubbard

Our world is abundant in beautiful and memorable places, regardless of which continent you have the good fortune to visit. I've been fortunate to visit four out of the seven continents, with only Africa, Antarctica and Iceland still on my bucket list of continents to explore. I believe it is also true for those three remaining continents that to really capture and understand the incredible beauty and uniqueness of those places, they have to be seen and experienced in person in order to fully appreciate the depth and meaning of what is on display.

With that in mind, and without a doubt, my all-time personal favorite destination in the world is the Hawaiian Islands. I've enjoyed so many wonderful visits over the years, more than twelve in total, during which I created a treasure trove of memories. Those are the kind of memories that were ingrained so deeply that I will never forget them. Even when my wife and I return after so many years, the memories come rushing back in to fill up our hearts, like we've never been gone.

I still remember my very first visit so many years ago at eighteen years of age, when I traveled to Honolulu at the invitation of a beautiful young lady. Although her home was in Honolulu, I met her on the mainland in southern California at a church summer music camp when she came to attend the two week program. Her name was Janice, but went by the name, Jan. That created a minor problem for me later when I dated a different girl the following year when I shortened her name from Janet to Jan. That is another story for another time.

When my younger brother, Mick, and I accepted her invitation to visit her family in Hawaii, we had no idea what to expect in this tropical paradise. I'd always wanted to go to Hawaii, but the cost and distance were a bit of a challenge. However, I really did like her and she was my motivation to generate the income and schedule the time to actually travel to the islands. I was too young and didn't know her well enough to say I was in love, but I did tell her "I am in like with you." She smiled approvingly and let me know she was okay with that.

When the plane touched down at Honolulu International Airport, we taxied to the terminal, but not quite all the way. Back in those days, the planes stopped just short of the actual terminal and we had to exit down the movable stairway that had been wheeled up to the plane door. Then we would walk on the tarmac the hundred or more feet to enter the actual terminal.

When the door of the plane was opened and as I passed through it, I was instantly hit with the warm, south Pacific breeze and the overwhelming fragrance of the tropics, such as I had never before experienced. In fact, this new and welcoming sensation hypnotized my senses and created a sensory experience and memory, greater even than I thought possible. It was magical. While walking down the steps, taking in the view of never-ending rows of palm trees, the lush greens of the distant mountains framed beneath the bluest of skies with occasional puffs of white clouds, I felt like I was descending into a whole new world and an experience that would stay with me all my life. But this was just the beginning.

As Mick and I entered the terminal, along with a hundred other passengers, we were greeted by lovely and beautifully tanned Hawaiian ladies, crowned with flowers and wearing their bikini tops and traditional grass skirts. In those days each new visitor was presented with a colorful and fragrant flower Lei. My beautiful friend, Jan, was also there to welcome us and presented both of us with another flower Lei. Mick, just two years younger than me, blushed when she kissed him on his cheek. I was quite comfortable with the kiss on my cheek, followed by a more enthusiastic and impassioned kiss I received on my mouth. What a great tradition!

After we collected our luggage, we got in Jan's car and headed to her home in Manoa Valley. All the way there, my head was on a constant swivel to see everything I could see and take in, and my mind was absorbing the incredible essence of the islands. Jan was the perfect tour guide and was amazingly knowledgeable on the sites of Honolulu, which she described in some detail.

As we moved up into the valley called Manoa, the area became greener and more lush with tropical foliage, and the intensity of the fragrance of the flowers was magnified. My senses were on overload trying to take it all in, with no attempt on my part to slow it down. It was absolutely incredible, and until I was there, fully immersed in the rapture of these island, experiencing and savoring its virtual buffet of sensual delights myself, I could never have fully understood just how special it was.

Over the next two weeks, we were able to travel all around the island, sometimes on our own, but usually with Jan showing us to all the best beaches for snorkeling, body surfing, and other places where most tourists don't know to go.

Jan's parents provided the regional leadership for the churches and ministries of our particular denomination throughout the Hawaiian Islands, so on Sundays, Mick and I attended church with the family. It gave us a unique opportunity to meet some local teens and many of Jan's friends. The Aloha spirit was clearly evident in their welcome and was greatly appreciated. It was like we were always friends and would be friends forever. The warmth was clearly Hawaiian.

On one particular day, a few of our local friends from church, took us up into the mountains to do "tea leaf sliding." I didn't know what that meant, but when we got up into the jungle, we broke off a branch of a tea leaf plant, sat on the leafy end, held on to the stem and started sliding down the mountain.

At first, trying to sit on the leaf and slide was challenging work as we forged our way down the hill, but every time we repeated the effort, the path got wetter and the mud increased. Each new ride made us go faster and farther as we followed the terrain and playfully struggled to avoid trees that were not about to give up their well-entrenched positions on the mountain side. Now, I can say that I once went tea leaf sliding. Not many can. It took the locals to show us this unique and exciting adventure.

We also wanted to try our skills at surfing for the first time ever. Since we were such surfing newbies, we felt it prudent to start with the gentle waves of Waikiki Beach. We rented boards and spent hours learning to choose the waves, attempt to actually get ourselves vertical and then ride the small waves in. It was a real exhilarating feeling to finally stand up on the board and make it all the way into the shallow surf along the beach. Then, we would turn around and paddle out to do it again.

Even when just sitting on the board waiting for the next wave, you could look in one direction and see the majestic and recognizably famous Diamond Head cratered mountain. Looking to shore, you saw beautiful hotels behind the sandy beach, including the historic pink Royal Hawaiian Hotel. Palm trees framed everything shore wide. Looking to sea, there were boats, sails, catamarans and an occasional cruise ship. There was so much to see, I would sometimes completely miss the next perfect wave.

We could have stayed there for hours every day, but we were warned that the sun is so much more intense out in the Pacific. If we had stayed out in the sun too long with our blonde hair and light, freckled skin, we'd pay for it later in a painful way. We were having such a great time, we forgot the warning, and were rewarded with a blistering sun burn. Oh well. Lesson learned.

We had the chance to experience a lot of things while in Hawaii, including the world famous Hawaiian dance show presented by Kodak. It was a wonderful performance with a variety of dances from the basic hula to the much faster and energetic Polynesian war dances. Guitars, ukuleles, drums and Hawaiian singers brought it all together. Everything you imagined the islands to be was represented in an intensely colorful show.

This dance show display was, in my opinion, "marketing genius" for Kodak because everyone was constantly snapping photos of the dancers and other performers, and most needed more film than they had brought with them to capture it all. The Kodak stand was close by and ready to sell the additional film to make sure everyone captured the experience. The lighting was provided by the sun, and the beautiful surf and sand of Waikiki Beach provided the backdrop for the show. Another picture perfect Kodak moment.

There was so much to experience on this adventure, and our new Hawaiian friends provided opportunities to do and see as much as possible in the time we had available to us. However, something was going on that I hadn't yet identified, but experienced on a daily basis on the island. It was so subtle that I didn't know what was happening, but there was something that seemed to elevate the value and quality of each new experience.

It finally dawned on me what I was feeling, and I fell in love with it. It was the warm and welcoming spirit of the local Hawaiians toward enjoying life. It was clearly revealed to me in a song performed by the iconic Don Ho at one of his shows. The song was called "Ain't No Big Ting Bruddah" and summarized for me a wise and wonderful way to face life and deal with the challenges it throws our way. The words to the chorus as I remember them are:

Ain't no big ting bruddah when things ain't looking up.
Ain't no big ting bruddah when there ain't no coffee to fill the cup.
Cause the good times coming, let em roll, let em roll.

The verses of the song focused on the tests and trials that life sends our way, and the repeating chorus reminds us of how to deal with them. It's that laid back, not-a-care-in-the-world attitude that says to me that life happens, but everything is going to be okay.

Regardless of what life throws at you, it "ain't no big ting brudda." The song has a fun and engaging tune that tends to stick in your head the rest of the day. Even if you don't remember all the words, you remember the chorus. The effect has you smiling with the tendency to wash away your troubles, or at least forget about them for a while and creates a renewed focus to enjoying life where you are. In Hawaii, you have the perfect reason to stop and smell the roses, and in fact, all the beautiful flowers there. Their all-pervasive presence amplified my senses to the point of total enjoyment and relaxation.

This may be an appropriate time to share with you that a few years later, I was enjoying a relationship with another Jan, formerly and officially, Janet. After graduating from college and being commissioned as a US Navy Officer, I married this Jan and we have been sharing our lives together ever since. So, from that day forward, when I travel to the islands, it is my "forever Jan" that shares the new memories we create together in Hawaii. Now, back to my story.

Don Ho was the master of Hawaiian song and became the first iconic performer and symbol of all things musical and representative of the island entertainment. His mellow and baritone voice, for me, set the standard for Hawaiian music and love songs and I will always remember how they endeared me to Hawaii and the wonderful memories created there.

Based on the numerous visits I've made to the islands since that time, I would be remiss to not mention that Hawaii is abundant with vocalists and other entertainers that have that special ability to engage the visiting tourists. Their sound is uniquely Hawaiian, and once you experience the deep and melodic music, you will undoubtedly agree with me that there is nothing like it anywhere else. It is absolutely that memorable, especially while enjoying a Pina Colada or a soft drink, the beautiful sounds of the islands and overlooking the sandy beaches and never ending, gently breaking ocean waves.

My wife and I love to listen to the songs of the islands, and our all-time favorite Hawaiian duo is the Chung Brothers, Es and Eddie. These masterful performers bring the music experience to life with the best of them, through their beautifully blended voices and unique entertaining style. We especially loved the way they engaged the audience with humor, stories, and an ability to make visitors feel like life-long friends.

We've been blessed to know Es and Eddie and the whole Chung family, and continue to enjoy their friendship as we have for more than forty years, and it is one that we shall forever cherish. I believe that is the magic of the uniquely Hawaiian "Aloha" spirit. I better move on before I get "sappy." You think?

For me, when I feel the need to escape the rigors and pressing challenges of life and get lost in a beautiful and magical place, Hawaii is where I go. It is the most incredible for me when my wife, Jan, is with me, and we reconnect with our island friends and are made to feel so welcome, again and every time. Yep. We are tourists and, Haoles, but we always feel at home with our friends. I hope that you will someday, if you haven't already, visit the Hawaiian Islands and create your own lifetime memories.

One last point I'd like to leave you with, a little personal secret of mine. This secret is a key component in my life and how I deal with the stresses and challenges encountered every day. I believe it is a collateral benefit to me in minimalizing the grey hair that is barely noticeable on my aging head. When necessary, and at any time I choose, I can escape to the solitude and renewing benefits of the Hawaiian Islands. That sounds great, if you can afford it, or even have the time to go. But, here is my secret.

The memories and experiences I have of the islands are so deeply ingrained in my mind, that I don't even have to go there. I do not have to physically be present on the islands. I just find a quiet corner of my home, my office, a booth in a restaurant, a bench in a park, or just about anywhere I am. I close my eyes and my mind transports me there, and I am reminded, regardless of whatever challenges I'm facing, I remember the special message of a song and know in my heart, "It ain't no big ting, bruddah," and all is well in the world again. It doesn't get any better than that. Aloha!

For Love of the Game

For many, sports in some form or another, is a very big part of our lives here in America. From the time me and my two brothers were able, our dad was teaching and encouraging us to play football, basketball, baseball and track. I know there were other sports, but these were the ones we were involved in with each of the seasons. Soccer was still little known in the United States or we would have been involved in that as well. Playing games was something we could do together and it provided all the benefits that come with sports involvement and being part of a team. We loved it, and dad did everything in his power to give us the opportunities to be involved in each of them.

Many, many years later when I was well beyond my prime, and retired, I was invited to get involved on the staff of a professional basketball team, the Vancouver Volcanoes. This was a real surprise to me because as much as I loved sports, I never imagined that I would have the opportunity of being engaged in such a way. When I was occasionally asked if I was a player, I had to acknowledge I was not, and in fact was kind of a silly question for me. But, I liked to respond with the statement that I was unable to play because I was too "SOS." I'd then explain that for me, it meant **S**hort, **O**ld and **S**low." Everyone would chuckle and we would move forward in the conversation.

Really, I was involved in my actual areas of expertise which were marketing, programming and sponsorships. This was a way for me to help this developing team and be engaged in a family friendly form of community entertainment. It turned out to be one of the most satisfying and fun periods of my life. To top it off, in one of our seasons, we won the Championship of the International Basketball League, and as a member of the Volcanoes team, I received a championship ring along with the players and coaching staff. At my age, who'd have thought that would ever happen? Honestly, not me. Today, that ring still sits on my display with other sports memorabilia I've accumulated over the years. Great memories.

By the way, the Vancouver Volcanoes was just one team associated with the International Basketball League. I learned that such teams and leagues existed all over the country and around the world to help developing athletes to continue to play in their beloved sport. These athletes were generally high level, former college basketball players who, for whatever reason, did not make the NBA draft, but wanted to stay in the game and continue to develop their skills and abilities. Teams like the Vancouver Volcanoes provided them a platform to continue doing what they loved to do.

These players were very skilled, and their passion for the game provided some of the best and most exciting community entertainment I have ever experienced. Unlike going to an NBA game where you can't get anywhere near the court, let alone close to the players, the action at our games was up close and personal. Then, at the end of the game, the players and the dancers would stay on the court to meet and greet the fans, including signing autographs, interacting with the children and posing for photos. This created a great fan experience for everyone, but especially the kids. We called it family friendly entertainment.

It made me proud to be associated with the Vancouver Volcanoes and the International Basketball League because it was a win-win environment for everyone, including the fans. In addition, some of our players would achieve a level of success where they were scouted by NBA teams, with some getting an invitation to try out or to play in some NBA summer leagues or attend camps. But, for many who didn't, they still had an opportunity to play professionally in other leagues around the world. This gave them continual growth, experience and an opportunity to play professionally, get paid and be superstars in other countries.

One of the admirable commitments made by our owner and coaches would be to help our players negotiate contracts to play in other countries and leagues around the world. Keep in mind, these are young men in their early twenties looking for opportunities to play, and we wanted to help them succeed in any way we could as an organization. On the court, these guys were as professionally skilled, aggressive and confident as you would expect of anybody at the NBA level. However, what I particularly enjoyed was how down-to-earth and relatable these guys were when off the court. They loved the game and it was so easy to be caught up in their passion and excitement of being a part of it all.

The team really played for the fans, a base of supporters that have grown over the years and were there every season to cheer on the team toward winning a league championship. One regular fan who attended over the course of four seasons was my father, a real sports enthusiast. Even at eighty eight years of age, he managed to get himself to the game every week during the season. I had a bench reserved for him and my mom, and occasionally a couple of their friends who would join them. I kept them close so I could occasionally join them in the stands, just to enjoy that time with them and share their enthusiasm for the game and their favorite players. It was a personal satisfaction to have them around and be so engaged, especially dad.

It was the final game of the final season that dad would be able to attend. He arrived early, as he always did, to not only be there to get his seat, but primarily to have a chance to speak to the players as they came in. As Josh Tarver, dad's favorite Volcanoes player, came into the gym, dad called him over. I was just down from the two of them as I was setting up the announcing table for the game. I overheard dad ask Josh how many points he was going to make that evening. Josh said, "twenty." So dad asked Josh if he would do him a favor when he made his first goal. He said to Josh, "When you make your first basket of the evening, would you turn and wave to me? That would be just for me and would mean a lot." Josh nodded his head and said he would. However, Josh had something else in mind.

Early in the game, as they came down the court, the ball was tossed to Josh and he approached the board and laid the ball up and in for his first two points of the game. As he came down from the board and started up court, Josh raised his arm and pointed directly at my dad, and continued pointing at him as he ran all the way down the court. It was an incredible salute to a fan, and an acknowledgement of the relationship that had been forged by this great player and his number one fan. My dad was so grateful and excited, and beamed throughout the night. I know that for a fact, because later that evening, he told me the story four times. His excitement and contagious smile were on full display. I believe it was the highlight of his Vancouver Volcanoes fan experience. It was also the last game dad was ever able to attend before he passed away later at age ninety two. I too, will never forget that game and the memory of the special gift I observed when Josh Tarver honored my dad in that special way.

I don't know that anyone else knew why Josh was pointing, or who he was pointing at, but I did. The way I see it is that, maybe even unbeknownst to Josh, it was a salute in honoring a man who loved the sport and had given so much of his life to playing, coaching, refereeing, umpiring, watching and supporting the traditions of sports in our lives. Dad knew the long traditions instilled by sports in building confident men and women, and how it makes this a better world.

Dad's relationship with Josh, as well as other players, was no surprise to me. I've watched him over the years and was always amazed at his ability to meet people and very easily relate to them, especially the younger athletes. He seemed to know everyone and was regularly encouraging them in their sport and how to excel in life. He always took time to speak to them, asking them how they were doing, and many times, would counsel them in decisions they were considering. I believe it was more the pastor and coach in him to genuinely care about each individual and offer guidance to each as they were willing to listen. I learned a lot from him and am proud of the man I called "my dad."

John Carr, my father and hero, will never make the Hall of Fame in Cooperstown or anywhere else, but in my heart, he is there already in my Hall of Fame for dads. If I was able to ask him why he gave and cared so much about sports, I am certain his response would be, "for the love of the game," and he meant it.

Mamma My Angel

"The human condition is the essential ingredient. It is only in the giving of oneself to others that we truly live."
Ethel Percy Andrus

There are many people in the world who believe in angels, and I happen to be one of them. I can't say that I have ever personally seen a "celestial being" as depicted in pictures, paintings or movies. However, I am a believer that they exist and they move among us.

I believe there are angels we do not see, but they are there. I also believe there are angels that we do see, and they are very much a part of our existence. Some angels are part of our daily lives and some just pass through our lives at a specific time of need. For me, I believe it comes down to faith and a belief there are forces in our lives that we do not understand, cannot see and many times, aren't even aware of. But, these forces, or angels, are there to help and guide us, maybe even protecting us in some miraculous way.

I have even wondered at times how close we may have come to losing our lives if it weren't for some divine intervention. I just don't know that answer, but there are numerous stories I've either heard or read over the years that suggest this has occurred.

One such story is chronicled in the chapter "Almost Gone Forever." But, there are numerous other stories as a child and growing up where incidents or accidents have occurred and I wondered how I ever survived. At the time, I'm pretty sure that I just shook it off as a coincidence, luck, or an arrogance that I am that good and that it turned out the way it did because of my own abilities. Maybe, or maybe not. Looking back, I'm still not sure. On a few occasions I recall either my mom or dad commenting something to the effect that they don't know how I survived childhood. I could tell you some of those stories, but not today. Let me get back to talking about the angels in my life.

One angel in particular that I believe played a crucial role in my life was my mamma. That may sound corny and could be passed off as a desire of my imagination and heart, but I can look back at our lives together and see all the incredible things she did for me. Those memories re-enforced my conviction that she was an Angel, not only for the way she guided, supported and encouraged me, but also for the sacrifices she made to make sure I was healthy, safe and secure. I believe she was chosen and sent specifically to watch over me because God knew I would need extra help to reach adulthood and manhood intact.

I like to think of my mamma as my real life, in my life, Angel. She was the primary loving, caring, understanding and patient influence in and around my life. She was always there guiding, directing and encouraging me. And, when I was ill, she was always there helping and watching over me while I healed and recovered.

I can't recall specifically any time when she ever got angry with me, but I've heard stories. I don't remember this one clearly, but when I was about four years of age, mamma was nine months pregnant with my younger sister. I must have done something, Lord only knows, but I understand she was chasing me around the house, she was so mad. I don't believe there was intent to kill, but fortunately, she wasn't able to get her hands on me. I ran into the bedroom and scooted up the ladder to hide in the corner of the top bunk bed. She couldn't reach me, but as she tried to scale the ladder, her good friend and our live-in babysitter, stopped her and helped calm her down.

Maybe Irene was another one of those angels in my life. To this day, I don't know what I did that made mom so angry, but I do imagine I probably deserved it. I wouldn't know this story except it was told to me on a number of occasions. Clearly, that phase passed and our relationship grew very close over the years.

I found myself in the hospital at age eleven just after we had moved to southern California. I was in a great deal of pain and the doctor diagnosed that I had a kidney stone. At that time, they decided the best way to get it out was to go in and get it. I won't bother you with the painful details of that effort, but rather I want to share another story of when Mamma, my Angel, made another willing sacrifice to provide comfort to a child in pain.

During the week I was in the hospital, I was waited on and cared for by professional nurses, special angels themselves. My room was clean and sanitized, meals were prepared and served, and all of my needs were met in a quick and efficient way. Looking back, I was pampered and spoiled for a whole week.

When I finally went home, I returned to my own bed in a room I shared with my two brothers. As I sat down, I started crying and mom asked me what was wrong. In my selfishness, I shared that the room was not like the one in the hospital and that mine was dirty and messy. I know for a fact that our house and our room was never dirty. It may have been messy at times, but even I knew that was because there were three young boys living in it, but our home was always meticulously clean. I'm embarrassed to share that at the moment, I was being selfish and ungrateful, and I knew better.

The fact that I was acting spoiled and selfish didn't matter to my mamma. She gave me a hug and reassured me she would make it better. In her kind and loving way, she immediately went to work on cleaning the entire room, not just my corner. Over the course of the next four hours, she put fresh, clean sheets on my bed, straightened up the room of stray clothing and toys. Then she got on her hands and knees and scrubbed the floor until it was cleaner than it had ever been. Then, she found a lamp and put it on an end table near my bed. When it was all done, she gave me fresh pajamas and tucked me into bed and placed a glass of water on the stand. She sat on the edge of the bed, gave me a hug and told me she loved me, always with a genuine and caring smile on her face.

I thanked her and hugged her back, and all was right in the world. It was her love and servant heart that responded to whatever was going on with me. I don't think I could ever thank her enough. I didn't deserve that kind of grace, but that was just who my mamma was.

There was another time in my mid-thirties when I was in the hospital following surgery for a hernia. Mamma came to visit me, which she did so many times over the years. One of the things I really loved about her was her sense of humor and energetic zest for life. I don't recall the conversation that started it, but it seemed that everything was funny, and we kept going back and forth, playing off each other.

I'd say something funny and she would come back with something funnier, and I responded with something else funny. When mamma started laughing, it was contagious and as the laughing increased, I began to feel the pain of the stitches in my groin. At one point, we were both laughing so hard, I had to press a pillow tight to my stomach in order to minimize the pain. However, it finally reached an unbearable point and I couldn't take it anymore and while laughing, I snapped "Get out!" "Get out!" Even that made us laugh harder as she headed out the door.

I was finally able to control my laughter, calm down and wait for the pain to subside. It finally did, and I could lay back, take a deep breath and relax. All was good, until I looked to the door, and there was mamma's head peaking around the door to see how I was doing. The smile on her face and the look of her peering around the door was so shockingly hilarious, it made me immediately burst into laughter again, press the pillow to my stomach and suffer through the pain again. It hurt at the time, but to this day, that is a wonderful and uplifting memory of my mamma, my angel, being in my life.

We were always laughing and enjoying life and family together, and I credit her heavenly spirit for having such a positive impact on me. When I was injured, she was there to help heal me. When my heart was broken, she was there to talk with me and assure me that everything was going to be all right. When I was angry or hurt, she was there to give me calm and understanding. When I was anxious, she was there to show me patience and perspective. When I failed in some way, she was there to let me know that failure is not terminal, and that part of living life is failing and then getting up to try again. And, when I was trying and succeeding, she was there to acknowledge and applaud my achievements, while at the same time, keeping me humble and down to earth. I could spend all day sharing stories like these, but that would entail writing another whole book with many pages.

I am so blessed to have had such a wonderful mother in my life over all these many years. I was also especially blessed by her patient, caring love and Christ-like influence which created the environment that prepared and helped me to strive in life and to become the man I am today. I have to admit she was loving to everyone who came into her presence, not just me. However, when I was with her, she made me feel like I was the most important person in her life. I'm sure she made others feel that way as well. Her love was boundless and I likely couldn't have made it without her. What makes me most happy and grateful is that I will always remember her as Mamma, my Angel.

Like A Rose
The many petals of Jan

"It's not your blood, your pedigree, or your college degree that matters. It's what you do with your life that counts."
Millard Fuller

In my humble opinion, the rose is one of the most, if not the most, interesting and intriguing flowers in the world, not to mention its captivating beauty. It is so amazing in all its many shapes, varieties and colors. Its fragrance is subtle, sweet and engaging as our senses are seduced and our memories are sparked to life with just a gentle whiff. Throughout history, the rose has also played a significant role in the lives of individuals, organizations and countries in ways that impacted both lives and nations, and therefore, history. I may be over-dramatizing their significance, but I don't believe I am.

Personally, I love the romantic mysteries and symbolic gestures that are represented by the rose, and I have happily engaged in the tradition by giving roses to certain lovely ladies over the years. My reasons varied from a desire to express a generous level of love, concern, compassion or encouragement by touching their lives in a visual and meaningful way. Sometimes, it was just to say, "I love you," or at the very least, "I'm in like with you."

Maybe I am old fashioned or what some would call more traditional, but my favorite color of a rose is red, although I've resorted to other colors or combinations when appropriate to the preferences of some individuals. I especially love the red roses just before they blossom and then as they open and reveal the really deep, dark and rich intensity of the red. It is possible that my preference for the red rose is because it was the very first one I'd ever seen and was captivated by its perfect combination of color, beauty and fragrance. Or, maybe it was how the roses were presented in various romantic movies, television or other media art forms that created such an impact on a young romantic. I don't know if I am a true romantic, but I've been told a few times that I am. I'm going to go with that. Whatever the reason, I really do love and appreciate the rose.

For me, the rose symbolizes my experience of growing and getting to know my life long partner, Jan. The simplest and clearest visual explanation I can think of to help explain what I am saying is that Jan is like a rose. She is like a rose in the sense that during our many years together, I was able to see and appreciate her multiple qualities and characteristics as a person, represented by each single petal of the rose known as Jan. Every petal identifies something new that I've learned about this unique and intensely beautiful woman, which is so much more than just her outside appearance. As this rose blossomed and the petals opened, I was amazed with the clarity and relevance of each petal. For Jan, she was just being Jan, but for me, I was developing an increasing appreciation for this deep and caring individual. How lucky can one guy get?

I was fortunate to find my "rose" when I was reasonably young and made the wise decision to marry her. It is unquestionably the best decision I ever made, and I am still, to this day, learning the value of that decision. When Jan was younger and growing into this amazing woman I was to learn so much more about, I had no idea the breadth and depth of what I was to discover about her, and from her, over the years. Let me share just a few examples of the many discoveries represented by each petal.

I had first met Jan at a church summer music camp for young musicians, which is where I got to know her and watch her grow as a musician over the years. She was learning to play the piano and the organ and clearly had a penchant for music theory and understanding of the notes and chords as they appeared on paper. That alone, put her light years ahead of me. However, I believe her greatest love and passion for a specific instrument came in the form of the tambourine. If your first reaction to that instrument is in the form of "so what" or "what's the big deal," I need to share more with you.

Most people only see the tambourine as a percussion instrument minimally used only to add some occasional rhythm sounds for a rock, country, gospel or folk group ensemble. However, in some circles, it is so much more. I won't go into its role in history as used by The Salvation Army, but when combined with their traditional brass band, it becomes an engaging and energizing component of the total musical message. To many in the audience, it is the most exciting and engaging visual effect. In this role, the tambourine is a "timbrel" and the musician is the "timbrelist." Sound easy? Oh, no it is not. These Timbrelists take the art form to a whole new level, learning their movements and choreography from carefully written scores to fit perfectly with the music of the performing band. The Timbrel Brigade, as it is known in The Salvation Army, is a well-trained precision drill team and is as effective and precise as any military drill team or sports cheer leading squads I've seen. What is key to any such successful team is the leadership, or in The Army vernacular, the Timbrel Leader. By the way, I also learned that a tambourine has one row of jingles and a timbrel has two rows. Who knew?

Through years of training and persistent effort, Jan became an expert on this instrument, to the point of not only playing the routines, but also composing drills and teaching these drills to other musicians, young and old. At the age of sixteen, to my knowledge, Jan became the youngest woman to be chosen to lead one of the top Timbrel Brigades in The Salvation Army world, the Los Angeles Congress Hall Timbrelettes. In addition, over the years, Jan was invited to lead clinics and teach this skill to other groups around the country. Jan credits her mentors and former leaders, Violet and Jeanette, for training and preparing her, and it was Vi who gave Jan her first leadership position. I have been amazed and proud of her ability to make this instrument an exciting and entertaining component of so many march numbers performed by various brass bands.

I share this story because it is just one of Jan's many petals, but also because I don't believe the leaders in this field have gotten enough acknowledgement for the effort and leadership it takes to make their presentations so spectacular and precise. Every instrument is important to the whole presentation, and the timbrel is no different. But, a well-trained, uniformed and precision Timbrel Brigade makes the entertaining experience so much more. That's the way I see it, and Jan made it so.

Another petal of Jan that I am so proud and happy to see in her is her drive and focus to learn, improve and grow in everything she does. When we moved from Texas to the northwest, Jan took a starting position within a major non-profit charity organization. You may be able to guess which one that might be. She started at the bottom as the secretary for the person responsible for all the properties of the organization over two states. In this position, she had to learn and develop her computer skills, understanding of contracts and other legal documents, as well as every other component of the property industry.

After years of learning and mastering her responsibilities and worth at her work, Jan was promoted as the assistant to the property department and eventually the leadership position as the Property Director at the division level. Due to her own efforts and commitment to serve her company, Jan rightfully earned this position and was rewarded by an appreciative boss. During this time, she even created the Property Guidelines manual used by all the entities in her two states Division, which was later adopted by the Western Territory corporate office and used throughout the thirteen western states. Jan could literally say that "she wrote the book."

Jan would sometimes lament that she didn't have a college degree which could have helped her in her advancements or acquiring other positions. However, as far as I'm concerned, and although she doesn't have the certificate obtained by attending and completing a degree from a university, I believe her knowledge and experience on property, construction, contracts and management is the equivalent of a Masters or maybe even a Doctorate degree in this field. She earned it in the trenches, I declare.

What is incredible to me, and what you don't know, is that she was a one person department for many years. She handled and was responsible for every transaction from buying and selling properties to every phase of each construction and remodel. Her projects ranged from hundreds of dollars to tens of millions of dollars. I don't know how she did it, but over her twenty plus years with the organization, she retained and could call at will every detail of every transaction for every property, and her historical knowledge made her invaluable in her position and to the organization. I was constantly impressed and in awe of her abilities and the depth of her commitment to making sure her service to her organization was more a calling and not just an occupation. Just another one of her amazing petals, and she did it meritoriously while being a wife and raising three wonderful children.

On another note, Jan once shared with me that it was her personal goal to see that every property in the Division was upgraded so The Army could better serve the people in need in those communities. Upon retirement, she was able to say: "Mission Accomplished."

My work took me on the road a lot, and I do mean a lot. Between my job and my US Coast Guard Reserves responsibilities, I have to acknowledge and credit Jan for mostly raising our children. Unfortunately, and to guilt I carry even to this day, she was left to head our home and hold our family together, which she did in such an incredible and servant way. I couldn't have asked for a greater life partner than Jan, and she did it mostly with a smile and without complaint while I was trying to build a career. It was my goal to someday be in a position to bring Jan home from work so she could enjoy life at home with the children. What it took me a while to learn is that she wanted to work. She enjoyed....no, she loved what she did. She had so much to give, and doing so energized her.

Jan loved being challenged and busy. Another petal came in the form of her commitment to serving through our church. Because it is such an important part of our lives, she also took on local leadership responsibilities including leading the Timbrel Brigade, the choir and our church's tape ministry to shut-ins and others who couldn't make it to church on some Sundays. To her, these were ministry callings, not duties. She loved it and was both capable and committed to serve, which was how she was raised and how she lives her life. It would be okay with Jan if only God knows. That is Jan. But, I know and so do many others.

Somehow, through it all, she still managed to parent our children and get them to their many doctor appointments, school activities and performances, fundraisers and numerous church programs. She also assisted their school dance team performances by helping the forty plus dancers with their hair and make-up requirements, all the while cheering their team on to state championships. At one point, we designated Jan as our "Wonder Woman." She certainly was. One year, for Halloween, she even dressed up as Wonder Woman and the kids loved it.

Over the years, starting even before we were dating, Jan was a "fit model" for a well-known swimsuit company in Los Angeles, and she continued in the field of modeling off and on over the years, including while we lived in Japan so many years ago. She became an instructor in modeling and skin care, keeping her hands in the entertainment industry in an occasional movie or television production, as well as helping other young models move their careers forward.

I believe she is also gifted in her humble way of counselling and encouraging those around her. Since, for a long while, Jan and I worked in the same organization, I was able to watch her develop and grow her subordinates to higher levels of responsibilities and leadership positions. In short, she is a servant leader with a servant heart, giving so much of herself to the success of others with little to no expectation of acknowledgement or praise. She does what she does because of who she is and I am so proud to be part of her life. I will even use the African word "Ubuntu" in my acknowledgements of Jan as she relates to me in my life. "Ubuntu" translates to: "I am, because of you." I use it because in my mind, "I am, because of Jan."

In this short chapter, I am not able to cover every petal of the amazing person I know as Jan, and in reality, she would actively be resistant to any attempt of me putting her in the spotlight. That is not her thing, and another reason she is such a God fearing, humble person. I live in constant amazement of this woman who knew way before me, that we would someday spend our lives together. Each new petal reveals yet another talent, skill or magical link to an expanding golden chain of qualities revealed in this gifted woman.

If I haven't made myself clear, although I'm confident you've figured it out, I love my forever Jan, and I would willingly give my life for her. In the meantime, I hope to have many more years to share with her and to continue to discover the petals of Jan that are yet to be revealed. Life with her has been fun, entertaining, challenging, surprising, mystifying and so much more. To cover all that would take a book devoted just to her. Trust me. I've been blessed in so many ways during my life with Jan. She is my rose.

Now, my wish for you is that you have found, or will find your own life long partner, your spouse, your own special rose, and together you will discover and enjoy the many petals as they reveal themselves along your journey. Remember, you are also a rose of many petals to your own spouse and the other people in your world. Enjoy the many "revealings" and may your life be abundant and full in so many ways along your journey. God bless you.

A Letter to You

Dear Friends,

Thank you for taking the time to read my stories. I hope you enjoyed them and each story found a jewel that was of value to your life. If not, keep digging. It is my desire that each lesson learned would be of inspiration and encouragement to you on your own journey through life. Or, that each story stimulated your thoughts and imagination, giving you something fresh to contemplate. For my part, I enjoyed sharing them with you.

You have a life, and a story, and I am confident there are those who may want to read it and learn from your lessons. If you choose not to write it, at least take the opportunity and speak your story out loud. You may never know the impact or influence your life has on those around you. Your knowing is not as important as the difference you may make in someone else's life. Plant those seeds and let the good Lord nourish them according to His will so they will someday bear fruit.

I wish you the very best in everything you do, accompanied with great success in those areas of life that are most important to you. May you step out and learn as many life lessons as you can, and may God richly bless you.

Sincerely,

Ron

Acknowledgements

There are a number of people I need to acknowledge who have made this book possible in some way, but I run the risk of missing or leaving someone out. Still, I want to attempt to express my gratitude, and if I miss you somehow, please forgive me and know how much I really love and appreciate you.

The original seed was planted by my mom, Peggy Carr, who listened to my stories and adventures over the years. It was she who first spoke the words, "You should write a book." In all honesty, my first reaction was, "Mom, you would be the only one to read it." Regardless, I finally began, and she was right. Many others wanted to read these stories, especially since each one provided a life lesson learned. As the book developed, there became so many more people I needed to thank, so here is my attempt to do that.

First, I want to thank my lifelong friend, Walt Waggener, not only for his very insightful and complimentary Foreword to this book, but also for being my high school and college best friend. Through those adventurous and discovery years, many stories and memories were created, most of which will never be repeated in any book.

I want to thank my good friend and mentor, Chuck Whitlock, who has been an inspiration for writing this book and for his support and encouragement over these many years.

I want to thank Jim Townley, another longtime friend, Coast Guard buddy, and the person who taught me the true meaning of Servant Leadership through his excellent example. I owe him big time for using his wordsmithing skills to masterfully edit this book.

Thank you to Joe Noland, another longtime friend whose love, prayers and friendship provided me numerous creative opportunities to be part of so many of his grand productions and programs. His challenges unleashed my growing skills and interest for the creative and performing arts.

Another good friend who has, and deserves, my love and appreciation, is Marilyn Clint for her friendship over many years, and for her constant encouragement and support while writing this book. She has been a cheerleader for me and this project and more as we worked together on so many not for profit fundraising efforts. Her creativity is an inspiration to learn what is really possible in developing an idea and sharing a message.

Thank you too, to my newest friend, Les "PeeWee" Harrison, whose smile, energy and enthusiasm are both inspiring and contagious, and whose words of endorsement regarding the impact of this book on his life, makes it all worth the time and the effort to put these life lessons in a book and share them.

I must also thank Esmond Chung, my Hawaiian friend and Navy Officer buddy from over forty five years ago. We first met in Japan while serving our country and have stayed connected all these years.

Thank you too to my long-time friend and former publisher, Jeanette Heinz, who provided guidance and enthusiastic support toward the completion of this book. She was another one of my special cheerleaders to whom I am forever grateful.

Finally, to my wife, Jan, who is my number one supporter, encourager and promoter. She has been instrumental in checking my work and allowing me the quiet space to create, while keeping everything else functioning in our home. And, she was always there when I just needed to talk and bring my thoughts into focus. She is my cheerleader extraordinaire.

To everyone who listened to my stories and encouraged me to put them down in writing, and whose enthusiastic support pushed me forward to completion, thank you. It is my prayer that this book will be everything you hoped it would be, and you can take pride in your role in me seeing it come to fruition. God bless you all.

Ron

Special Announcement
Be on the lookout for
"Crooked Sidewalks Too"

This follow up book will share more of Life Lessons Learned with fun stories, relatable topics and more lessons learned with topics like the following:

Someone's Hero	My Hidalgo	Best Laid Plans
Aortic What?	Cruisin' Alaska	Darn the Deck
Direct Hit	Finding Reasons	Pass in Review
Meatloaf Messenger	Olympic Task Force	Tres Arroyos
Ross and Margot	Got Regrets?	Easter Sunrise
My Friend, the Servant Leader		(.......And more)

For additional information, or to check his speaking availability, you can contact Ron directly at his book email:

CROOKEDSIDEWALKSBOOKS@GMAIL.COM

About the Author

After graduating from the University of La Verne with a degree in Biology, Ron entered his second summer of training at the Naval Officer Candidate School in Newport, Rhode Island and was commissioned an Ensign on November 5, 1971. After Viet Nam service aboard a Navy Destroyer and later an Aircraft Carrier, he ended his active duty commitment. Yet, three years later, he resumed service as an officer in the US Coast Guard Reserves and eventually retired after twenty two years of service.

In civilian life, Ron was a uniquely skilled writer, establishing himself for over 30 years as a marketing, public relations and fundraising professional for government and non-profit organizations. Early signs of a developing talent became evident in his early childhood as he began to distinguish himself as an engaging story teller, creative spirit and skilled communicator. Ron's trained listening and discerning skills, along with his sensitive and caring demeanor, helped him to share his personal stories with humor and realism in order to engage his readers in a personal and meaningful way.